MY JOURNEY SO FAR ...

Lessons on Life from Fellow Travellers

MATT SUMMERFIELD

EDITOR

Authentic

Contents

Introduction

It was late 2003, and my friend Chris Curtis and I were getting our money's worth at the local 'all you can eat' pizza joint. During the hour or so we spent over lunch that day, I shared with Chris a challenge that we were seeking to address within Crusaders. Crusaders has been working as a missionary movement amongst youth and children across England, Ireland, Scotland and Wales for nearly a hundred years. The Crusaders leadership team focuses much of its time and effort on envisioning, equipping and encouraging the thousands of volunteer leaders who run the 450-plus local groups across the UK and Ireland every week. Over the last few years we had significantly 'raised our game' in the provision of resources and training, culminating in the launch of a pioneering new package called 'Energize' which seeks to deliver high-quality, flexible meeting plans and training for work with five- to eighteen-year-olds for every week of every year. But something was missing ...

We were providing some fantastic new resources that would enable men and women to be more effective leaders of youth and children, but deep down I knew that we had to do more than that. I knew that we also had to find some creative ways to encourage these leaders in their own personal walks with God. Meeting plans can only go so far – more than anything, young people need relationships with men and women who have a dynamic, ever-deepening knowledge of and love for God. Jesus himself makes it clear that the most important thing we do is to love him with everything we have. So therein lay our challenge. What could we do as a movement to encourage and inspire the faith journeys of our volunteers?

I've always been a great believer in the language of 'journey'. The psalmist reminds us in Psalm 84:6 that those who set their hearts on pilgrimage are blessed. Every day we continue to travel – learning and growing – seeking to become all that Jesus intended for us to be.

As we discussed our own faith stories over lunch that day, Chris suggested that it would be valuable to hear about the personal faith journeys of other Christians. We could ask them questions such as: What have they learned so far? How are they developing their relationship with God? What do they love about God and his words? What advice could they give to fellow travellers?

Such honesty and vulnerability might help the leaders in Crusaders to remember that life is a journey through which we're all still learning. We need to be real about the fact that we all struggle at times. The journey isn't always easy. Perhaps the example and advice of some would help other Christians in their own pilgrimages. Most of us are familiar with sharing our stories of coming to the faith, of how God rescued us. But what then? What about the years of perseverance, puzzlement, even persecution, that follow? What we envisioned is a sort of twenty-first-century *Pilgrim's*

MOST OF US ARE FAMILIAR WITH SHARING OUR STORIES OF COMING TO THE FAITH, OF HOW GOD RESCUED US. BUT WHAT THEN? WHAT ABOUT THE YEARS OF PERSEVERANCE, PUZZLEMENT, EVEN PERSECUTION, THAT FOLLOW?

Progress, with stories to encourage saints today on the journey along that narrow path.

So, as our lunch came to an end, the idea of *My Journey so Far* was born. We decided that every month we would provide our leaders with a new article on our Energize website, giving honest reflections from a fellow Christian traveller on the joys and the challenges of living out the Christian faith. The resulting web-based series was unique and proved so popular that our friends at Authentic picked it up and decided to publish it – the result is in your hands.

In developing the 'My Journey so Far' series we were keen to receive reflections from a broad range of people – from well-known leaders of Christian organizations to lesser-known heroes who face the daily challenge of expressing their faith in a non-Christian environment. Everyone has a story to tell! As you read, you will see some of the kaleidoscope of God's creativity reflected in the very different viewpoints, faith experiences and backgrounds of the contributors – all members of God's family experiencing his love and grace in unique ways. Many of the stories here also remind us of the humanity of our Christian leaders, who don't enjoy being put on pedestals and are ever aware of their frailty and weakness.

I HOPE THAT THIS BOOK ENCOURAGES AND CHALLENGES YOU IN YOUR OWN JOURNEY.

I hope that this book encourages and challenges you in your own journey. Some of the people in this book reflect upon specific questions we asked them; others share their life stories and reflections on the journey in a slightly different format. This volume is ideal for 'dipping into' – when you have ten or fifteen minutes to spare, take a moment to pause and read the story of a brother or sister in Christ. Many of us feel isolated and alone, thinking that everyone else has got it 'more together' than we do. The truth, however, is that none of us have got it 'all together'. As you read these stories I hope you'll be reminded that we all wear 'L' plates until the day we die – the day when we shall see him face to face, when we shall be like him, when we shall see him as he is.

In the meantime, enjoy the journey of discovery.

MATT SUMMERFIELD
Executive Director
Crusaders

Matt Summerfield joined Crusaders as Executive Director in May 2000. Prior to that he was an IT manager at the mobile telecommunications company One2One (now T-Mobile) for ten years. He is an associate pastor at Hitchin Christian Centre, which is a member of the Pentecostal denomination New Testament Church of God. Matt has been involved in youth and children's ministry for over 16 years, primarily supporting local church and schools but also speaking at national and international youth events on occasion. Matt is passionate about effecting a level of change that will result in the rising generation of children and young people being released into their full God-given potential. Matt is married to Jo and they have two sons, Andrew and Daniel.

Foreword

CHRIS CURTIS

Talking to myself?

> To come to what you know not,
> You must go by the way where you know not.
> To come to what you are not,
> You must go by a way where you are not.
>
> – St John of the Cross

Do you ever talk to yourself? I sometimes imagine what it would be like, you know. Not to the 'me' of the here and now (though it has been known to happen). But to the me of twenty years ago, a youth worker in Bristol. I was just starting out in 1984 (1984? I always thought that was a slightly worrying year to start trying to instruct teenagers in the Christian faith – from an Orwellian point of view).

I imagine the two of us (or should it be the two of me?), sitting over a coffee in some cafe near the docks in the city centre. What would I want to say to the younger me? What advice would I want to give me? What dark holes would I want to help me avoid?

I'm not sure I like this idea, though. For one thing, the journey hasn't been all bad and there really isn't much I'd want to leave out. After all, it was usually in the tougher times when I learned things – either about myself or young

AFTER ALL, IT WAS USUALLY IN THE TOUGHER TIMES WHEN I LEARNED THINGS – EITHER ABOUT MYSELF OR YOUNG PEOPLE – AND SOMETIMES EVEN IN THE WORST MOMENTS. people – and sometimes even in the worst moments. So perhaps the advice to me would be 'Go for it! Get out there, make mistakes and experience it all for yourself. You don't need me to stop you falling down a hole. Fall away, and see what you learn on the way down, at the bottom – and on your way back up again!'

Maybe there's a deeper reason I feel uneasy with advising my youthful self. I know that I'm still working through many of the issues I wrestled with back then. I never managed to quite sort them out. How can I tell the young me to read the Bible more, pray more or whatever else, when I know I'm still facing the struggles of those disciplines twenty years on?

Although I can't quite see the value of my own advice, I know that I am who I am in Christ today because of the many who helped me on the way. I can see some of those friendly faces – older and wiser youth workers who offered advice and kind words when I needed them. They were an important part of my journey. Even though I've forgotten some of the particulars of the advice they gave, their presence was important. At the very least, they reminded me that it was possible to make it. There was a time when it seemed like all the youth workers I knew were leaving youth work – often out of frustration with their churches, or because their marriages were crumbling under the strain of so many evenings out. There were even some who, because of these and other pressures, found that their faith was going off the boil. At times like that, it was good to meet people who were in for the long haul and who still showed passion and zeal for their faith and young people. Sometimes you need to be reminded that they're there, to hear their stories and words of encouragement.

Jack is one of those people who has encouraged me in this way. He's fast approaching sixty, still a full-time youth worker, and his love for God and teenagers seems as bright as ever. He's a living, breathing lesson for me. He doesn't keep up with fashion, and he probably has no idea what kind of music young people are listening to, but teenagers love Jack. When you see him around them, you understand why. He listens. He's never in a hurry. He pays attention to them like they're telling him their deepest secrets, even when they're talking about little of any consequence. Life has taught Jack that there will always be other planning meetings, strategy days and deacons' meetings. They play second fiddle to being with a young person who wants to talk. Show up at Jack's house unannounced (how many teenagers keep appointment diaries, after all?), and you know you'll always get a warm welcome. You won't ever feel like you're just an item on his 'to do' list. You're not a target of his youth strategy, and you're not ever going to bore him with your stories and musings. Someone once said that being a Christian was never about becoming more spiritual, but about becoming more human. Jack has a way of making people feel more human.

SOMEONE ONCE SAID THAT BEING A CHRISTIAN WAS NEVER ABOUT BECOMING MORE SPIRITUAL, BUT ABOUT BECOMING MORE HUMAN.

I wish I'd been more like Jack from the start. I was often so target-orientated that I forgot to just hang out. I was busy trying to double the size of the group, but in the process I often forgot to show each young person how valuable they were. I should have stopped more often and done 'nothing' with the young people with whom I was working. Teenagers are, after all, experts in the art of doing nothing for large expanses of time. (Can you imagine reporting to the church your new plan to

do 'nothing' with the young people as often as possible?)
Ironically, it's during those times of doing 'nothing' that
we often get closest to the heart of what 'youth work' is
really all about.

Jack taught me that my cool games, clever Bible studies
and nifty video clips amounted to nothing if I didn't add
the missing ingredient of love. And love, in a teenager's
terms, is about time.

If you ask teenagers whether their parents love them,
they will often reply in terms of time: 'He only ever sits
down with me when he wants something.' 'My Dad never
takes me anywhere.' 'She's always there for me.' When
you ask parents about their love for their children, they
often reply in terms of provision: 'I wash his clothes.' 'I
give him a lift when he needs one.' 'I pay for her dance
lessons.' I realize now that I often saw things the same way
as these parents do. I wish I'd spent more evenings kicking
a football round the park, watching videos or sitting on
the grass on a summer's evening chatting about nothing
until it was time to go home.

Jack isn't the only youth worker who made an impression on me over the last couple of decades. I learned much
from Phil, too. Phil is one of those youth workers who is
as excited about his own faith as he is about being a youth
worker. Now that might sound like an obvious thing to
say, ridiculous even, but here's what I mean. Phil took as
much time to develop his own journey with God as he did
to encourage young people to begin their own. I always
sensed that Phil never let his youth work get in the way
of his faith. The two weren't joined at the hip, if you know
what I mean: take away the need to study the Bible or pray
specifically for youth work, and you'd still have something
left. Phil studied the Bible even when he didn't have a Bible
study to prepare! He was a great challenge to me in those
early days to keep feeding my own faith.

I guess Phil was showing me what Jesus meant when he reprimanded Mary for her busyness while Martha simply sat and listened. I love that story in Luke 10. And I need to hear it again and again because I know that I find it so much easier to plan what to do in next Friday's youth group than to sit and listen to the voice of Jesus speaking to my own life.

Back then I thought that Phil's passion for Jesus simply made his Bible studies and youth work even more luminous and effective. I realize now that it wasn't Phil's Bible studies that made such an impression on the young people he worked with – it was Phil himself. He was one great big living Bible study that spoke to teenagers in ways that probably he himself never realized.

I wish I'd paid more attention to that now. I still struggle to grow in my own faith, outside of what I do, but at least I feel more aware of the challenge. In the early days, I don't think I saw things with such clarity.

I remember, too, meeting Andy in those first years. He challenged me with how much of himself he gave away. I can think of several meetings I sat in with Andy, along with other church youth leaders, planning some local event or celebration. In those meetings, we would often discuss what names would be attached to the publicity or who would lead an event. Andy would never push himself in those moments. He didn't have to prove himself the 'best' or more 'successful' youth worker in the town. His was a far less personal ambition than most of us had. He would be the first to give away a great story or illustration and the first to draw others into what he was doing.

Andy saw his work in kingdom terms: he was secure enough to see beyond his own church's boundaries while the rest of us were busy trying to impress each other. If his event clashed with that of another church, he would be the first to withdraw and throw his heart into someone else's venture. I wish now I'd been able to let go of some of my unhealthy ambition and worry a little less about whether I was the best or worst youth worker around. I wish I'd seen beyond the walls of my own church a little more often. Andy brought the phrase 'preferring one another in love' out of the pages of the Bible and into our lives.

So maybe I would have something to tell my younger self, sitting at that cafe drinking coffee. I wouldn't want to have missed either the highs or the lows of the last twenty years. Like I said, I've probably learned more from the lows. But I would want to challenge myself to look around and learn from others. Jack's passion for young people, Phil's passion for God and Andy's heart for others have all had a huge impact on my life. Of course, although they were around me, I didn't always stop to see what I could learn from them. I realize now just how great God's grace has been in my life. Despite my blindness to some of these great truths, God still used me. This is the mystery and glory of serving God – that out of our weakness he is still glorified. I thank God for his grace, and for the people he put in my path. I hope that you, too, will learn about God through the people you meet along your journey.

> THIS IS THE MYSTERY AND GLORY OF SERVING GOD – THAT OUT OF OUR WEAKNESS HE IS STILL GLORIFIED.

Chris Curtis lives and works in Luton, where he hangs out with young people as part of his job with the Luton Churches Education Trust. He says he learned more in the first month of parenting a teenager than in 20 years of being a youth worker. He spends a dangerous amount of his time watching movies and on the internet.

Getting into Intimacy with God

EMS HANCOCK

We caught up with Ems, a Proverbs 31 girl-in-training, while she was taking some time out from juggling her roles as wife, mother, writer and youth leader.

> *Ems, as you reflect on your journey so far, what would you identify as some of the big life lessons God has been teaching you?*

While I grew up in a loving Christian family, I also had to deal with some difficult experiences. I was the victim of a number of instances of sexual and physical abuse, and these left me questioning lots of things about myself and about the world around me: What was it about me that made these things happen? Does it happen to everyone? Like many people who have come through a background of abuse, I have had to learn to accept myself. It's a slow process of understanding that what has happened cannot be taken away, and instead allowing God to heal the memory of it.

IT'S A SLOW PROCESS OF UNDERSTANDING THAT WHAT HAS HAPPENED CANNOT BE TAKEN AWAY, AND INSTEAD ALLOWING GOD TO HEAL THE MEMORY OF IT.

I knew from a very early age that God was real and that *he* loved me, but as I grew up – because of the way some people had treated me in my childhood – I often wondered how or why *other people* could love me. As a young teenager I felt I didn't deserve friendship and loving relationships with others. I suffered from low self-esteem and to a certain extent excluded God while I tried to deal with the problems I had. I used to daydream about someone coming to rescue me and whisk me away.

The summer I was sixteen, however, God intervened and did something really dramatic in my life. My grandmother took me to a big Christian conference in the Lake District for a holiday. I was immediately struck by the number of cool people there – people who made me feel accepted and liked, and who, more importantly, demonstrated so openly and passionately a faith in God. One of them was a twenty-year-old leader called Steve, and I got on especially well with him and his girlfriend – they were amazing, and their strong relationship with God was inspiring. I was actually quite envious of what they had. One morning we talked about heaven, and Steve told me that he wanted to be an artist when he got there. We laughed about the fact that he couldn't even draw a stick man.

Later that day, we walked past a stall selling Christian T-shirts and I bought one (it was actually hideous) that said 'Don't be caught dead without Jesus'.

I was wearing the T-shirt that afternoon when we went down to the lake. Steve took some young people out to swim to the little island in the middle of the lake.

Right before my eyes, he drowned.

By the time they pulled him out of the water there was nothing anyone could do. He had died. Two things flashed through my mind ... the wording on my T-shirt, and the thought that Steve had just become an artist in heaven.

In that moment, I understood in a way that I never had before that death is not the end, and that life has purpose and meaning – however much we are hurt in that lifetime. God spoke to me clearly in the coming months, challenging me to live 100% for him, and it radically impacted how I felt about myself and dealt with the issues of abuse from my past.

> *What aspect of the nature of God causes you to stand back and think, 'That's awesome!'?*

I have always thought, and still do, that the most incredible thing about God is that he completely disregards my sin. It's not that he forgets it. Forgetfulness is a human trait. Rather, God *actively chooses* not to remember what I have done to offend him and others. When he looks at me, he doesn't see a sinner, but he sees a Saviour – his own son. That blows my mind.

A man called Mehmet Ali Agca shot Pope John Paul II in 1981. The Pope needed hours of surgery and weeks of rehabilitation to recover from the shooting that could so easily have robbed him of his life. In 1983, the Pope paid Agca an unexpected visit in his prison cell. Agca was amazed to hear the Pope say, 'I have pardoned you and you have my complete trust'. The man must have thought he was dreaming!

I think this Christ-like forgiveness is one of the most awesome marks of spiritual maturity people can have. I once interviewed a man whose daughter had been raped. It

I THINK THIS CHRIST-LIKE FORGIVENESS IS ONE OF THE MOST AWESOME MARKS OF SPIRITUAL MATURITY PEOPLE CAN HAVE.

was a privilege to meet this man. Again and again he assured me of his prayers for her attackers. He didn't hate them, but he prayed that God would change them. I found it so inspiring to hear that, and it challenged me to treat people who have hurt me the same way. No matter how big or small the hurt may be, my aim is to live a life of daily forgiveness instead of bearing grudges.

Can you tell us how you're growing in intimacy with God? How do you connect with God in the midst of life's demands?

When I was at university, I was fortunate to be mentored by a Benedictine monk called Father Theo. He spent a great deal of time with me, recommending books and asking me questions about my reading. Father Theo taught me to pray thoughtfully and led me through ancient techniques of connecting with God through biblical meditation. Since then I have tried to go away by myself regularly for times of retreat and silence. This has enriched my ability to hear and respond to the call of God. There are times when I have heard an audible voice, telling me to do something. At other times I have received a sense of direction that seems to come straight from God's word.

For the last 15 years or so I have kept a prayer diary, and this has become a valuable tool in my walk with God. In it I record what I am praying for and what God is saying to me about specific situations from his word. It is a huge privilege to have this record of the things God has done in my life, and I'd encourage every Christian to keep such a diary because it's so easy to forget what God tells us and what he has done in the past.

Whenever I find myself doubting God, or circumstances cloud my ability to focus on him, I go back to my diaries and find again the truth of John 10:4: '... the sheep follow him because they know his voice.' Intimacy with God is the thing I most crave. There is no greater privilege than walking closely with God and I hope it's something I continue to grow in and become better at until the day I die.

What's your favourite passage in the Bible, and how are you applying it?

My favourite passage in Scripture is Proverbs 31:10 onwards, describing what it is to be a godly wife. I find this passage constantly challenging and stimulating as I seek to live in a way that blesses my husband, family and friends. The woman in these verses is incredible. She works diligently and provides for everyone around her. She is resourceful and wise. She brings prosperity and blessing and people trust her completely.

I recently asked a friend to pray with me on a monthly basis – that I would be able to live up to truths like this in God's word. Over these last months, I have been consistently challenged to go the extra mile in my prayers and relationships, in my practical giving of time, energy and ideas. I have a long way to go before I can say I'm a Proverbs 31 girl, but I am on the journey.

Ems, what one piece of wisdom from your own journey would you like to share with your fellow travellers?

I find that one of the most difficult roles in leadership is that of delegation. Often those who are used to being leaders find that it's quicker and easier to do things themselves, but it's not necessarily the best way of encouraging, exciting or blessing others. I have learned – and am still learning – that God calls leaders to enable others to lead. This is the kind of leader I want to be.

It can be frustrating to watch people making mistakes or saying unwise things. But Jesus models this for us beautifully in the relationships that he had with his followers. Never did he say, 'Oh, for heaven's sake! You're doing it wrong!' And if ever anyone was entitled to say that, Jesus was. Instead, Jesus was a patient teacher who let those around him serve, heal, perform miracles, argue, question him, lie, fish, make mistakes and let him down. There's so much we can learn from him even as a leader of people.

I learned the hard way that delegation is the best way to lead. Several years ago I took a team on a Christian holiday. I had planned every minute of every day – it was all organized and ordered. I had only been there a few hours, however, when I realized that, far from pleasing God, I was squeezing God out. I was not using the gifts and talents of those who were with me. I had a humbling few days (with a very gracious team) as I faced the fact that I needed to change my approach to leading. It took me some time afterwards, talking through that mistake, to learn how to lead others more effectively.

FAITHFUL LEADERSHIP IS OFTEN ABOUT BEING A SERVANT YOURSELF.

Faithful leadership is often about being a servant yourself. It's not glamorous and it doesn't give you much status or power. The leader should often be the one in the background, taking none of the glory. Jesus left the company and majesty of heaven to be born in an undignified feeding trough. He really knows what he is talking about when he models this style of leadership, doesn't he?

Next time you are tempted to do something yourself, ask the Lord to show you someone else who might benefit from doing that particular task. You might be surprised at who pops into your mind. The circumstance might just allow you to witness the birth of a proper disciple, rather than a spectator Christian who can never be as wise, funny, prepared or gifted as you are.

Ems is married to Jon and lives near Tunbridge Wells in Kent. They have one boy, Sam, and identical twin boys on the way! Ems trained as an infant teacher but has worked as a freelance writer for a number of years. She co-leads the worship with Jon at their church, and they are both involved in the youth programmes of Spring Harvest.

Take a moment to reflect on what you have just read. What one thing do you want to remember and apply in your own journey?

How will you 'get into intimacy' with God?

40÷5

ANDY HICKFORD

Andy has spent just over 40 years on his journey so far, more recently as a minister, author, teacher and father. Here he shares five key lessons to help you on your own journey.

At the time of writing I am five months into a mid-life crisis, having recently turned forty. The fact that my eight-year-old son is trying to place my childhood alongside the things he is learning at school has not helped my state of mind. 'Were you born before or after the great fire of London?' was not a question I found encouraging. In keeping with this stage of life I have been reflecting on the lessons I have learned along the way. I hope that these thoughts from my experiences will give readers a few pointers for navigating their own journey of faith.

In acceptance lies peace

I can never remember a time when I did not believe in Jesus. There were many times when I tried hard not to, but it was no use – he was always there. It got to the point where I couldn't think about anything seriously anymore because I knew I was living a lie. Eventually I gave in. I became a Christian – and very miserable I was about it, too. Later, I was again seriously unhappy when I became aware that God was not going to settle for my chosen career option in law. To my horror I began to realize that God wanted me instead to be a minister. As I turned my back on university and applied instead to Bible college I genuinely thought this was going to be the end of my happy life.

On both occasions though, I was, in the famous words of C.S. Lewis, 'surprised by joy'. I simply could not have imagined the freedom I would experience when I started to be obedient. It was exhilarating. I was learning an important lesson. In acceptance lies peace. He knows best, he can be trusted.

IN ACCEPTANCE LIES PEACE. HE KNOWS BEST, HE CAN BE TRUSTED.

Accountability

I was a slow learner, however. Even after three years at Bible college I was still trying to put off the inevitable by exploring teaching as an interim career. It was then, while I was trying hard to avoid God's call to ministry, that I learned another life-changing lesson. I spoke to people who I deeply respected and who had been influential in my life and asked them to advise me. They never conferred with each other but were blunt and unanimous. Ministry it was.

It was then that I started to learn the value of account-ability. All of us need others who will speak into our lives the things that we would rather not hear or that we cannot see. This lesson has been so important for me that I would now say that I do not believe in personal holiness anymore. We are only able to live as God planned with each other's help. I remember speaking to my minister about going out with the woman who is now my wife before I even mentioned it to her! It was yet another situation in which I knew there was no way I could hear from God objectively. I needed others.

I have learned, too, that you have to be proactive to achieve this level of relationship. It does not just happen. You have to be intentional about it, inviting others you trust to speak into your life. We have to give people permission to ask the intrusive, to question the motives and challenge the behaviour. As a leader this is a vital part of my life. I can only have authority if I am subject to it. Accountability is a profound statement about God's ways being higher than mine and about trying to follow him in humility.

Smart guidance

After receiving such an unequivocal call I spent the next ten years of my life as a youth minister in Luton. When eventually the time came to move on, my experience of guidance was very different. While the first time it had been really clear, this time I prayed and fasted and sought to be accountable – and God appeared to say precisely nothing. I found it very unsettling. It felt like I was on my own.

I have heard an awful lot of rubbish on the subject of guidance. You may have heard it too. It generally goes along the lines of, 'Do A, B, C – and hey presto!' I have learned that the way God guides is much more sophisticated. It's important to understand that when we ask God what he wants us to do next, he has a number of concerns.

First, he wants to use this season of uncertainty to make us more like Jesus. He guides, but not in a way that by-passes our intellect, experience, willingness to listen, or our need to learn from our mistakes. All of that is about developing our character, making us more like Jesus. We want information – he wants character.

Second, he wants to use the indecision to develop our trust in him. We want a road map – he wants relationship.

So God is in the business of guiding us – my journey has convinced me of that, but it very rarely feels like it at the time because he is doing other things with us too. Guidance is normally a rear-view mirror experience.

GUIDANCE IS NORMALLY A REAR-VIEW MIRROR EXPERIENCE.

Lifelong crosswords

After 18 years of leadership in the local church and literally thousands of conversations with people from up and down the country about faith, I am intrigued to see how all that has shaped and changed me. For example, I think I am learning to live with more and more questions these days. As a teenager growing up in the church I was taught that Christians were custodians of 'The Truth'. I even remember going to a conference in London called 'Absolute Truth'. The idea was that Christianity was true and our job as the church was to proclaim and convince others of that truth. Over the last 20 years I have learned something very important. Truth is not a concept, he is a person. Jesus is the truth and his ways are higher than ours. 'We see but dimly' as Paul so eloquently put it.

These days it's as if I am constantly revisiting my faith. To love God with my mind means that I am continually questioning, re-evaluating and learning. My understanding of faith is like a crossword. I used to believe that 2 across was this and that 3 down was that – but now that 5 down is this, 2 across can't be what I used to think it was.

Chastened boldness

Alongside a growing list of questions, I see something else happening to me. Ever since the Son of God changed the history of the world by being crucified, real spiritual power has come in weakness. In our weakness, God's strength is revealed.

When I was younger I imagined that by this stage of life I would be moving confidently into my most productive phase of life, building on the foundations of the past with still plenty of energy for the future. While I probably am doing those things to some degree it certainly does not feel like I thought it would feel. With every year that passes I feel more vulnerable, more uncertain and more doubting of my own capabilities. But here's the strange thing. At the same time I feel bolder in faith, more secure in God's love for me and more ready to take risks in leadership. These days, Jesus is bigger. It's as if I am learning to expect less of myself but more of him. I can do all things through him who gives me strength. I can only call it a chastened boldness, a growing distrust of myself going hand in hand with a growing wonder at the gracious purposes of God.

> I CAN ONLY CALL IT A CHASTENED BOLDNESS, A GROWING DISTRUST OF MYSELF GOING HAND IN HAND WITH A GROWING WONDER AT THE GRACIOUS PURPOSES OF GOD.

So there it is. Forty years of journey condensed into five sound-bite lessons. Now to find my son and convince him there is life in the old dog yet!

Andy Hickford was the youth minister at Stopsley Baptist Church in Luton for ten years. He was involved in innovative work and became a regular contributor and consulting editor of *Youthwork* magazine and a regular speaker at national youth conferences. Since 1996 he has been the minister of Maybridge Community Church in Worthing, Sussex. He is the author of *Whose Life Is it Anyway?* (Worthing: CPO, 1994) and *Essential Youth: Why the Church Needs Young People* (Milton Keynes: Spring Harvest/Authentic Lifestyle, 2003). Andy also teaches and preaches at events like Spring Harvest, Soul Survivor and New Wine and serves on the board of Tearfund. He is married to Cerys, and they have three children.

Take a moment to reflect on what you have just read. What one thing do you want to remember and apply in your own journey?

How would you divide the years of your journey so far according to the lessons God has taught you?

Passion for People: God's and Ours

FRAN BECKETT

Fran took time out from the daily demands of her work with the Church Urban Fund and church planting to share some reflections on 'the bigger picture' of how God is at work.

Fran, as you reflect on your journey so far, what would you identify as some of the big life lessons God has been teaching you?

God is much bigger, more purposeful and more radical than I tend to give him credit for being. We quite rightly trust in those Bible words that say there is a consistency in his nature so that Jesus is the same today, yesterday and on into the future. But this doesn't mean that we can box him in with our assumptions and insecurities, minimizing him to be only as big as we think he is. Quite the contrary. God demonstrates an outrageously generous unpredictability when he does the totally unexpected,

GOD DEMONSTRATES AN OUTRAGEOUSLY GENEROUS UNPREDICTABILITY WHEN HE DOES THE TOTALLY UNEXPECTED, TURNING AROUND SITUATIONS AND PEOPLE IN WAYS WE NEVER BELIEVED POSSIBLE.

turning around situations and people in ways we never believed possible. We cannot sanitise him or tame him or make him fit below the ceiling of our faith. He is so much bigger and more loving.

When leaders have a small view of God, this affects how they approach their leadership responsibilities. We say that we're dependent on God, and in many ways that may be true. But often we behave as if it's all down to us, and when we come on the scene God can start getting on with the task at hand. God is, of course, already at work before we get there. Our role is to try to discern how he's working and get on board in order to co-operate with him. How often do we make our plans, ask God to bless them, and then carry on regardless without taking the time or having the humility to enquire what he's already doing?

Leadership can be demanding, exhilarating and at times quite lonely. Being in Christian leadership is an enormous privilege, and I enjoy it immensely – yet sometimes the weight of it can feel debilitating. This is particularly the case where there isn't shared leadership responsibility. People often look to the leader for vision, the answers to sometimes unanswerable questions about why things go wrong, or just expect the leader to constantly be on top of things because they think that's what Christian leaders do! At times like these especially I need to have a grip on the truth of the bigness of God and know that he's got things in hand, even when it doesn't look like it, and I need to remember that we human beings are the junior partners in it all. This perspective can remove the unnecessary burdens I sometimes try to carry on my own.

What aspect of the nature of God causes you to stand back and think, 'That's awesome!'?

Many of God's characteristics cause me to catch my breath in amazement, but the one that is particularly on my mind currently is his creativity. Sadly, the evangelical wing of the church has not always emphasized the application of the doctrine of creation to our understanding of everyday life but has instead used it more often to refute theories of evolution. But as we read the Scriptures, consider the world around us, look up at the stars and see God's creativity mirrored in people's lives, it is absolutely mind-blowing. God's ability to bring life, order and beauty out of nothing that we read about in the Genesis account is amazing. I marvel at his attention to the tiniest detail, and also at the enormity of scale that transcends human comprehension. God has created marvellous variety, colour and shapes.

The beauty of creation provides a striking reminder that God loves the world he has made – and what's more, he gives us the responsibility to look after it. Recognizing God's handiwork in creation helps me to understand more about his character and actions, and this knowledge stimulates increased confidence in my everyday interaction with him. Creation challenges us to release the creativity that he has put into people made in his image, and to celebrate the colour and vibrancy of the life he has brought into being. It also reminds us, accustomed as we are to communicating Christian truth through words, that we can connect in other ways – using images and other forms of creative expression – with a post-Christian society that is largely sceptical about institutional religion.

Can you tell us how you're growing in intimacy with God? How do you connect with God in the midst of life's demands?

Christian leaders need to be more honest about the fact that growing in intimacy with God is not always easy. And we have to be honest with our God and with ourselves. For many of us, Bible reading is usually related to the next talk we have to give and much of our prayer life consists of urgent 'please bail me out' prayers. We can look like we've got it all sorted, as we give the talks and advise others on cultivating their relationship with God. Inadvertently, this results in us modelling and perpetuating a form of Christian discipleship that is more about activity than relationship.

To grow in intimacy with God we need to grasp deeply, at more than head level, what it means to be his much-loved child. Christian leaders need this knowledge in order to lead not out of insecurity or a drive to find identity, and in order not to be threatened by others who appear to be more successful. I need to go back regularly to those verses in the Bible that speak of this love and chew them over again, asking the Holy Spirit to write them into the core of who I am. There are seasons when I write rather than speak my conversation with God – usually when I'm finding things tough going or I've lost direction or purpose. And I now block out two long weekends of retreat time in my diary every year. These times give me space to reflect, pray, read, listen to God and 'recharge my batteries'. The principle of carving out space like this is important, but how we go about it will differ according to our circumstances, commitments and personalities.

> TO GROW IN INTIMACY WITH GOD WE NEED TO GRASP DEEPLY, AT MORE THAN HEAD LEVEL, WHAT IT MEANS TO BE HIS MUCH-LOVED CHILD.

What's your favourite passage in the Bible, and how are you applying it?

I have often spoken on Isaiah 58 over the years, and these verses never fail to excite me and give me fresh vision. This passage speaks eloquently of God's passion for people. It is also a call to whole life discipleship, to experience intimacy with him not through outward religious show but through expressing God's own passion for people. Isaiah 58 also encourages us, promising richness in relationship with God as we pursue his agenda in a world that desperately needs the church to *be* good news as well as to speak it. This passage, and others on a similar theme, have inspired me over the years to envision, teach and train Christians in community action; to be involved in it myself; and to lead organizations working this out in practice – like the Church Urban Fund where I currently serve. Out of this same conviction, too, I lead a church plant in Peckham in south-east London called 'Restore', which is bringing God's passion for people to an area with profound problems yet amazing potential.

> *Fran, what one piece of wisdom from your own journey would you like to share with your fellow travellers?*

I enjoy the innovating, shaping and pioneering aspects of being in leadership, and possessing a certain drive and conviction about the rightness of what I'm doing is essential to my effectiveness. Being intentional about how I lead my life is important to me. But the danger is that this sort of drive can lead to an unhealthy independence, as we become set in our ways about how we get things done and become isolated from others. Sometimes I can feel the success of a particular venture is all down to me or I can become impatient because people aren't doing things the way I think they should be done. Being the one who leads, whether in a Christian setting or not, does set one apart from those who are being led. In light of all this it is absolutely essential to risk investing in building relationships with godly people who will be there for me and hold me to account when necessary. I hear too many tragic stories of leaders who have burned out and cracked up or become so discouraged that they've just quietly withdrawn into themselves. There also can be casualties among those on the receiving end of inappropriate leadership 'ministry' from leaders who have little or no accountability to others.

All of us, regardless of our stage of life or whether we're in leadership or not, need to be accountable to others in order to be well rounded and mature

> WE ALL NEED PEOPLE WHO PRAY WITH US AND FOR US, AS WELL AS RELATIONSHIPS THAT WILL STIMULATE, STRETCH, TEACH AND ENCOURAGE US.

godly Christian people. We all need people who pray with us and for us, as well as relationships that will stimulate, stretch, teach and encourage us. In all of this, we should never forget to enjoy the fact that God enjoys us. With all of our frailties and individual quirks he is so for us, in a way and to a level that goes far deeper than even that of our closest friend.

Formerly Chief Executive of the Shaftesbury Society, Fran has a background in local authority social work, Christian student work and urban community development. Fran is now Chief Executive of the Church Urban Fund, which supports Christian social action in the poorest areas of England. In her spare time, she leads 'Restore' – an urban church-planting initiative particularly committed to 'being good news' and discovering ways of reaching people who see the church as irrelevant.

Church Urban Fund (www.cuf.org.uk)
Restore (www.restore-peckham.org)

Take a moment to reflect on what you have just read.
What one thing do you want to remember and apply in
your own journey?

How does, or could, your life reflect your passion for
people?

Finishing Well

GERALD COATES

Writer, speaker, broadcaster and leader of the Pioneer network, Gerald feels strongly that the private lives of leaders cannot be separated from their public profile ...

Gerald, why do you think it's absurd to try to separate the private and the public?

I say this is 'absurd' because we would never accept that the private life of, say, an alcoholic surgeon has nothing to do with his profession. Nor could the private life of a paedophile be separated from his teaching primary school children. Somebody addicted to heroin would not make a good taxi driver.

One of the major lessons I have had to learn, and continue to learn, is that it is vitally important for leaders to keep their public and private lives as close together as possible. When I look back over my journey so far, these two people (my public self and my private self) have at times had barely a nodding acquaintance with each other.

If the public and private spheres of our lives drift apart it will not be long before we have to start covering up our private inconsistencies, indulgences and sins that have become a way of life. Invariably the sins we employ to disguise the original wrongdoing are as bad, if not worse.

> *As you reflect on your journey so far, what would you identify as some of the big life lessons God has been teaching you?*

Having just celebrated my sixtieth birthday, finishing well is the big thing for me. Both of my parents died of heart attacks at the age of fifty-three, so I am doing rather well. But I want to continue to learn, to grow closer to God.

I don't think leaders who fail, or fall, understand the huge effect this has on the average Christian, and particularly on the young. This is true of those who lead house groups, cell groups, children's or youth work and local church leaders as well as of Christians in business, arts, entertainment, medicine and education. People are watching.

LEADERS OFTEN GET BURNED OUT OR TIRED; THEY REACT TO CRITICISM OR TAKE JOURNEYS IN THEIR PRIVATE LIVES UPON WHICH THEY SHOULD NEVER HAVE EMBARKED.

Leaders often get burned out or tired; they react to criticism or take journeys in their private lives upon which they should never have embarked.

Kill a shepherd and the sheep are lost.

Many start well but finish badly. My parents were God-fearing but not regular church goers. I was brought up in Cobham in Surrey, 20 miles south-west of London. At around the age of five I was sent to Sunday School, where I learned about Jesus' birth, life, death, resurrection and ascension, as well as his teachings. This gave me a good basic foundation. When I was nearly twelve, my cousin invited me to a youth camp where I heard the gospel and understood that I could do more than merely know about God – I could actually know Christ and have him in my life. This changed everything.

Through my teenage years I conveyed in public what I wanted to be but discovered a lot of things about myself in private which were to lead to struggles, cover-ups and shame.

When I was seventeen, I was riding a motorbike that got a puncture, went out of control and clipped the kerb. I shot over the handlebars like a rocket out of a silo. My head hit a brick pillar. I was blinded in one eye and broke most of the bones in my body. I was rushed to hospital, where the doctors discovered that five clots of blood surrounded my brain. I was given four hours to live. My parents were told I would not survive the night and were sent home. I was unconscious for a week and semi-conscious for another, but I came through. Just as God had put his hand on my life when I was nearly twelve, he did it again at the age of seventeen.

After this experience I began to attend the only evangelical church in our small town, which gathered in the Gospel Hall. For six or seven years I was taught a high view of Scripture. In this congregation we followed a simple approach to worship – though we did think we were right and everybody else was wrong. Having been spoiled by good Bible teaching, I realized that the God who did great things did not appear to be doing much in the late 1960s. Our church was afraid of Pentecostals and we knew very little of the charismatic movement which was predominantly within the Anglican church anyway, led by Michael Harper and the Fountain Trust.

One day, while riding on my bicycle, I began to sing in a language I had never heard.

When the church leaders found out, they graciously told me that they could not have this in the church. So my wife and I had to leave. A few folk gathered around us, and over the next few years we became a centre for hope, healing, the baptism in the Spirit and buildling relationships.

Thirty years later, I am now leading a UK-wide network called Pioneer which encompasses nearly a hundred churches, training initiatives (including DNA, now in partnership with Crusaders) and a number of ministries including those of Jeff Lucas, Delirious?, Noel Richards, children's worker Duggie Dug Dug, Sue Rinaldi and Pete Greig of 24/7.

God has also given me many opportunities to share the gospel in different contexts. I have spoken at conferences all over the world, have written a number of books and have had my own TV show and radio programme. I have appeared on BBC and ITV on numerous occasions and edit *Catalyst*, a journal of teaching and news primarily for the Pioneer network. I host the Round Table of Charismatic Evangelicals, work with OFCOM/Central Religious Advisory Council on maintaining and improving ethical and religious output and am an advisor to several in politics, entertainment and publishing.

I share all of this not to blow my own trumpet or to inform you of how busy I am. Profile doesn't equal importance any more than lack of profile equals non-importance. Rather, I share all of this because God has been unbelievably kind to me, despite my flaws and failures. While all of this is demanding, it is also wonderfully satisfying and I love telling stories about people I have met, things I have seen and lives that have been changed.

The weakness of deriving satisfaction from these things is that it is only a step away from self-satisfaction

– just as being righteous is a step away from being self-righteous.

So another big lesson I've been learning is that I need to be continually aware and on my guard – especially when I am tired, depressed, overworked or feeling deprived or undervalued.

In the world of science, negative energy travels faster than positive, so I continually remind myself that we reflect what we focus upon. This is why I tell my positive stories.

IN THE WORLD OF SCIENCE, NEGATIVE ENERGY TRAVELS FASTER THAN POSITIVE, SO I CONTINUALLY REMIND MYSELF THAT WE REFLECT WHAT WE FOCUS UPON. THIS IS WHY I TELL MY POSITIVE STORIES.

What aspect of the nature of God causes you to stand back and think, 'That's awesome!'?

I have always had a fairly good understanding of God as my father. But when I read Luke 15 (the parable of the prodigal son), I realize it should be called 'The Parable of Missing the Point'. Jesus tells three stories – about a lost sheep, a lost coin and the lost son. And when that son in that well-known story returns home repentant and indeed rehearsing his repentance speech, the story switches to this amazing father. Because while the son is confessing that he is not worthy to be a son but is returning as a servant, it is clear that the father is not listening – he's planning a party. And indeed, in all three stories, celebrate, celebrate, celebrate – or party, party, party – is the point Christ was trying to get across to the serious religious scholars of the day.

What Jesus Christ was saying is that God is not a judge but a dancing father, a partying father, a relational being, who invites us to party and dance with him – despite the fact that we've blown our inheritance.

Of course fathers have to bring judgement, that is what they do, but it is not what they are. Love is his essence, judgement is what he does.

Can you tell us how you're growing in intimacy with God? How do you connect with God in the midst of life's demands?

We sustain our relationship with Christ through reflection, prayer (both structured and spontaneous), and particularly through relationships (where we connect with God in other people and benefit from their insights, love, care and wisdom).

I also find a deep connection when I am prophesying over people and seeing their response. I have an email on my desk right now from somebody in Switzerland who said that when God gave me some words for him, his whole life changed, has been cleaned up, and crooked ways have become straight.

What's your favourite passage in the Bible, and how are you applying it?

My favourite passage, one I return to regularly, is Ephesians 3:8–21. Paul is talking to his huge church about what he is endeavouring to do when he preaches and teaches, how he responds to the grace of God, and he declares that 'Christ will live in you as you open the door and invite him in.' He finishes with:

Glory to God in the church!
Glory to God in the Messiah, in Jesus!
Glory down all the generations!
Glory through all millennia! Oh yes! (*The Message*)

Eugene Petersen has done a fabulous job in translating the Scriptures and I would encourage every young person to read *The Message*. It is so liberating and life-transforming – and so accessible.

> *Gerald, what one piece of wisdom from your own journey would you like to share with your fellow travellers?*

If I could give any piece of advice to other Christians, and particularly to leaders, it would be '*Forgive!*' in all situations. Being a leader means you have some sort of profile, for me it has been much higher than I could have dreamt. I've had tremendous opportunities to be a spokesperson in the media and for causes such as March for Jesus, Pioneer and the Aids initiative ACET.

But leaders (whether local, national or international) are often unaware that such a high profile can unintentionally breed jealousy, envy, gossip, lies, half-told truths, competitiveness and sometimes outright hostility. Because I have been so much in the public eye, inevitably I have said things I should not have said and probably left unsaid some things that should have been said. While I feel I have not been wholly undeserving of some of the backlash, I have learned that forgiveness is the key to moving on with laughter in our hearts and smiles on our faces to embrace the Dancing Father.

Gerald Coates has been married to Anona for almost 40 years. They have three grown sons who live near them. Gerald leads the Pioneer network of churches based in a dozen different nations and is a speaker, writer and broadcaster.

Take a moment to reflect on what you have just read. What one thing do you want to remember and apply in your own journey?

In order to 'finish well', Christians need to be able to practise forgiveness. How do you need to apply that truth in your own life?

Making Today Count

JOHN BUCKERIDGE

John, influential Christian leader and editor of *Christianity* magazine, urges us to look beyond the tyranny of the merely urgent ...

John, as you reflect on your journey so far, what would you identify as some of the big life lessons God has been teaching you?

I have the initials TTT written over my computer – this stands for 'things take time'. I'm fairly impatient and want things to happen today, right now. I also tend to get bored quickly, and so perseverance – seeing things through to completion – is an area that God has been working on in my life.

The most notable example of that occurred around my fortieth birthday. Throughout my thirty-ninth year I sensed that God wanted to speak into my life when I reached forty. During this time I felt very unsettled. I had pioneered the launch of *Youthwork* magazine several years earlier but the publishing company was transferring to a new owner and I was wondering if it was time to move on myself.

I was at church on the Sunday nearest my fortieth birthday. That day we had a visiting preacher, Gerald Coates, who heads up the Pioneer network of new churches. Halfway through his sermon he stopped, looked at me and started to prophesy about my future. I was so surprised and embarrassed that I didn't really take it in at the time. However when I got the recording of his talk I wrote down what he said. I still have the piece of paper – I keep it in my wallet. Part of the prophecy was, 'I feel God would say to you, "Don't give it away, John." People give things away too soon. Sometimes the fight is too tough and the course is too narrow and we just feel it's time to move on. But whatever God is speaking to you about ... you mustn't give it away.'

I knew that God was speaking to me about my involvement in the magazines – and specifically *Youthwork* magazine. That prophetic word encouraged me to stay committed to the vision of equipping volunteer and salaried youth workers through a monthly magazine. In 2004, seven years after I received that 'word' to stay put and 'see it through', and 13 years after editing the very first edition, I handed over the reigns as day-to-day editor – although I continue to have an oversight role as editorial director of *Youthwork*.

The ability to pioneer something new is important – but it's even more important to take things through to maturity and to empower someone else to take things further after you leave. Sadly, finishing well seems to be a rare commodity in the Christian ministry.

THE ABILITY TO PIONEER SOMETHING NEW IS IMPORTANT – BUT IT'S EVEN MORE IMPORTANT TO TAKE THINGS THROUGH TO MATURITY AND TO EMPOWER SOMEONE ELSE TO TAKE THINGS FURTHER AFTER YOU LEAVE.

Often those who work with young people are good at starting things off but sometimes fail to see it through. Being there for the long haul, staying faithful to your calling – that has become more and more important to me.

> *What aspect of the nature of God causes you to stand back and think, 'That's awesome!'?*

It's hard to isolate just one. Everything about God makes me think 'Wow!' But I guess if I had to choose just one thing it would be his sovereignty. He is in charge, and I need to let God be God in my life. I find that hard, as I am fairly independent. I have a tendency to try and pigeon-hole God – to try and work out how he works and then limit him to certain patterns of behaviour. But slowly, oh so slowly, I am learning that God is God. Isaiah 55:8–9 puts it perfectly:

> 'For my thoughts are not your thoughts, neither are your ways my ways,' declares the LORD. 'As the heavens are higher than the earth, so are my ways higher than your ways and my thoughts than your thoughts.'

God has the right to do and say what he wants and, though it is good to learn about his ways, and it's helpful to study theology and church history, God is bigger than my understanding.

> *Can you tell us how you're growing in intimacy with God? How do you connect with God in the midst of life's demands?*

This question presumes that I am currently growing in intimacy with God. I find it difficult sometimes to tell if I am going through a time of spiritual growth and intimacy. Looking back over time it's easier to identify fertile or fallow times.

I am coming to understand that a sense of closeness with God can sometimes go – and it may not necessarily be because I have given up on spiritual disciplines. I believe that we go through different spiritual seasons. There have been times of 'summer' in my life when it seemed like I couldn't have been closer to God. Other times it has been spring – a time for planting, for sowing, for giving away, for investing in the future. I have also experienced autumn – times of mellow fruitfulness – when God has answered prayers in miraculous ways and encouragement has been around every corner. So far in my life I have not really experienced a spiritual winter – but I know others who have – and I don't think it's been because they were necessarily disobedient or walked away from God. Rather, for whatever reason, they have not experienced the close intimate presence of God for a season.

I like variety, so I haven't found one book, one set of Bible reading notes, one worship leader or preacher or one style of meditation or spiritual discipline that always helps me to come close to God. One thing I do consciously cultivate in my life that helps me to experience the closeness of God, and may help others as well, is 'thankfulness'. I try to remember and be grateful for all that God has done for me – and this process of 'counting my blessings' warms my heart, builds my faith levels

I TRY TO REMEMBER AND BE GRATEFUL FOR ALL THAT GOD HAS DONE FOR ME – AND THIS PROCESS OF 'COUNTING MY BLESSINGS' WARMS MY HEART, BUILDS MY FAITH LEVELS AND REMINDS ME OF THE MANY REASONS I HAVE FOR BEING CHEERFUL.

and reminds me of the many reasons I have for being cheerful.

What's your favourite passage in the Bible, and how are you applying it?

'The thief comes only to steal and kill and destroy; I have come that they may have life, and have it to the full.' (Jn. 10:10)

I love preaching about this 'fulfilled life' that Christ promises his followers, and I daily try to live in the truth of it.

As well as being a good reminder that Christ wants to give me a fulfilled life – which doesn't necessarily mean comfortable or happy – this verse also cautions that I have an enemy. Satan and his army of demon angels hate me and want to destroy me. So without getting paranoid and imagining that there is a demon behind everything bad that happens to me, I am aware that just as I have a Saviour who loves me and wants me to be fulfilled, I have a mortal enemy who wants me to fall, get depressed, cynical, lose hope and fall into addictive and sinful habits. Most of the time I don't see anything of the principalities and powers who are battling over my life and the lives of others around me – and that's just as well, I guess. But I do try to be aware of the spiritual climate I am in and ask God to help me to be sensitive to his Spirit

I walk over the river Thames twice a day as I walk from Vauxhall station to the offices where *Youthwork* gets edited. As I walk over Vauxhall Bridge each morning I try to focus on the day ahead. I ask God for his help and remind myself I am in a war. On my way home, I ask God as I walk over the Thames to help me leave behind any stress or strains from the day so I don't take that back into my home, where I want to spend time with my wife and two sons. I also thank God for another fulfilling day. I want to be full and filled with God's Spirit – that way I know I will be fulfilled. I also want to be alive and alert to the enemy of my soul.

> *John, what one piece of wisdom from your own journey would you like to share with your fellow travellers?*

'Make today count' is a good motto to live by. I meet so many people who seem to be living in anticipation of something they don't have. Our society is built on making people dissatisfied with what they have so they will buy new stuff on a credit card or aspire to a better job or bigger house or whatever. But enjoying the moment, seizing the opportunities today brings, squeezing all the fun, hope and life out of 'now' is so vital – and it's quite counter-cultural. The alternative is dissatisfaction and living for tomorrow – except tomorrow never comes, because there is always something more to strive for.

'MAKE TODAY COUNT' IS A GOOD MOTTO TO LIVE BY. I MEET SO MANY PEOPLE WHO SEEM TO BE LIVING IN ANTICIPATION OF SOMETHING THEY DON'T HAVE.

This way of living can revolutionize your attitude to people, things and the time you give to different things. Making today count isn't about short-termism or failing to plan for the future, nor is it about hedonism and the pursuit of pleasure. Rather, it's about having an eternal perspective, not taking tomorrow for granted and prioritizing my time. Make today count.

John Buckeridge is the editor of *Christianity* magazine and the editorial director of CCP Ltd, which publishes the magazines *Youthwork, Christianity* and *Christian Marketplace*. He was the founder editor of *Youthwork* in 1991.

Take a moment to reflect on what you have just read. What one thing do you want to remember and apply in your own journey?

How will you make today count?

Walking with God

DEREK TIDBALL

> The Principal of the London School of Theology says that he feels 'like a kid setting out on a long car journey, driving his parents to distraction by asking, "Are we there yet?".' He says, 'My journey began a long time ago, but I'm definitely not there yet. One day I will be ...'

The start of the journey

I thank God for the fact that my parents were committed Christians. They were not preachers or up-front leaders and never made a great public display of their faith, but it was very real for them and permeated every part of their lives. I thank God, too, for my early training in the faith and in my knowledge of the Bible in the churches they took me to, first in a little Gospel Hall and then in a thriving Baptist church. The next step, for me, was to take that secure 'Sunday School' faith and test it out in the revolutionary student world of the late 1960s. Would it stand the tests thrown at it by my fellow sociology students and by my atheist professors in the militant Marxist context of the day? I went back to basics – to

Jesus. And, sure enough, it stacked up. Jesus could be trusted and was worth trusting with my life.

Finding the way

The road since has contained a number of unexpected twists and turns. As an impatient young man I wanted God to give me the map of my life so I could get on with it, finding the road and changing direction when the map led me to do so. I used to think it would be so much easier if God would show me the next ten years ahead. I suppose I thought I could relieve him of the responsibility of having to look after me. But then I discovered that the Bible never promises that God will give us the map – only that he will prove to be the guide. Psalm 32:8, for example, says, 'I will instruct you and teach you in the way you should go; I will counsel you and watch over you.' That meant I had to keep closely in step with him and depend on him to lead me for the future.

BUT THEN I DISCOVERED THAT THE BIBLE NEVER PROMISES THAT GOD WILL GIVE US THE MAP – ONLY THAT HE WILL PROVE TO BE THE GUIDE.

This is just as well, because map reading is not as easy as it sounds and I am sure I would have taken a number of wrong turns. After teaching for a year I set out to Bible College to train as an itinerant youth evangelist. Most of my experience in evangelism and in leadership at that time had come through BYFC, so it seemed a natural development. But God had other plans and guided me – through addresses I heard, wise counsel I received and prayerful reflection – into local church ministry. To cut a long story short, I ended up pastoring a church and teaching evangelism part-time at my old college (London

Bible College, as it was called then). God, the divine guide, knew what he was doing. I had studied sociology at university but never expected to use what I had learned. Although I didn't know it at the time, when Gilbert Kirby asked me to join the staff of LBC he anticipated that in a few years they were going to want someone to teach sociology as well as evangelism. God's ability to take the messy, diverse threads of our lives, including what we consider to be loose ends, and weave them into a coherent pattern has never ceased to amaze me.

To cut an even longer story short, I found myself teaching at LBC, pastoring in churches and working as Secretary for Mission and Evangelism for the Baptist denomination. In 1995 it was a delight to be called back to lead LBC (now the London School of Theology) as Principal. God, in his providence, had prepared me well over the years. He knew the range of skills and relationships I would need in place to meet this new challenge.

> GOD'S ABILITY TO TAKE THE MESSY, DIVERSE THREADS OF OUR LIVES, INCLUDING WHAT WE CONSIDER TO BE LOOSE ENDS, AND WEAVE THEM INTO A COHERENT PATTERN HAS NEVER CEASED TO AMAZE ME.

Just as God had prepared me vocationally, he also sovereignly directed my personal life. Dianne and I knew each other quite well through LBC, then lost touch for a bit, before we got married. At the right time, God brought us back together. Our son, now an enthusiastic Crusader, almost certainly would not have been born had God not engineered our lives to be near a great hospital where they offered some adventurous medical care just when it was needed. God's providence is writ large in our lives.

Trusting the Guide

In Scripture, Jacob is the arch-fixer. He's always manipulating, positioning himself for the advantage and seeking to be in control of his life. My testimony is that we will only mess things up if we seek to do that. Our lives are much better in God's hands than they are in our own. At the end of his life Jacob spoke of God as 'the God who has been my shepherd all my life to this day' (Gen. 48:15). Pity it took him so long to work that out. Pity he hadn't trusted God's shepherding skills earlier in his life. Trusting in God takes the strain out of life. It doesn't make us apathetic, negligent in preparing ourselves or in taking responsible decisions. But it does mean we can prayerfully move forward believing that God will lead us and that he is bigger than any mistakes we make. The crucial thing for a Christian is to trust God.

A companion on the way

What's the secret of sustaining over 30 years of Christian ministry through many exciting and prosperous times as well as through patches that have been hard or merely routine and monotonous? The secret is walking with God. One of my favourite Old Testament characters is Enoch. Little is said of him except that 'after he became the father of Methuselah, Enoch walked with God 300 years' (Gen. 5:22). I've sometimes wondered whether the writer who penned these words connected his walking with God and his fathering of Methuselah deliberately. Was it because the child was difficult to handle that Enoch was driven into the arms of God? Be that as it may, Hebrews tells us a tiny bit more about Enoch. His life was lived 'by faith' and 'pleased God' with the result that he bypassed death and went straight into the eternal presence of God (Heb. 11:5–6). The companionship he had enjoyed regularly, but no doubt interruptedly, here on earth was replaced with a companionship that was permanent and uninterrupted in the 'afterlife'.

What does it mean to experience such companionship with God? It must mean obedience, for there can be no pleasing God when we are flouting his will. But it's more than that. Walking with God points to a quality of relationship that Enoch enjoyed with God. Though they were never equals, and could not be, they obviously enjoyed each other's company. How do we get to know God like that?

For me, the old-fashioned spiritual discipline of the daily Quiet Time has been crucial. I begin each day (well, most days!) intentionally with God. I need to do it at the start of the day when I'm free from people, from phones and email, and even free from family. Space and quiet are vital. I take a little time to focus on God in prayer, then read a passage in the Bible – systematically, not randomly or haphazardly – then pray. I'll often read notes or a commentary alongside the Bible, but I change this periodically to avoid predictability and to keep it fresh. Currently, most of my college community and I are working through Scripture Union's *Essential 100* together. This provides us with plenty to talk about during the day. It's great doing it together.

Into the mix of my Bible reading I always put a psalm or a chapter of Proverbs. January 1 always sees me reading Psalm 1 – a great way to start the year. That means I can read the whole of Psalms and Proverbs twice during the year. My prayer time is a conversation with God. Though I've kept a prayer diary and tried to be systematic in praying over the years, I've never maintained those patterns for long. Prayer for me is conversation, and conversation leads to companionship. As time goes by, this strengthens one's walk with God immensely and we begin to think biblically when we meet situations during the day and can often use Scripture to bless or help direct others as well as ourselves.

The effect of his companionship

All Christians, and leaders in particular, often find themselves giving out to others. The reservoir can run dry unless we take steps to replenish the supply regularly. Of course the Holy Spirit, who renews us day by day, is the primary source of refreshment (2 Cor. 4:16). But the Spirit will often work through our Bible reading and by connecting our feeble prayer words to the living God. Some people think that it must be either God working in us by his Holy Spirit, so we need not do anything, or, our own effort in disciplined prayer and Bible reading. But we should not drive a wedge between the two. God works both directly in our lives and indirectly through good spiritual routines like daily Bible reading, prayer and witnessing.

I often want to ask young Christian leaders how they are going to give to others if they have not taken in for themselves. Occasional Scripture reading and the odd chat with God, when we feel like it, is not enough to keep our spiritual reservoirs full. We'll quickly run dry without a daily time with God. And, when we practise this, walking with God throughout the day becomes so much more of a conscious delight.

> I OFTEN WANT TO ASK YOUNG CHRISTIAN LEADERS HOW THEY ARE GOING TO GIVE TO OTHERS IF THEY HAVE NOT TAKEN IN FOR THEMSELVES.

Walking with God shapes our character. Friendships involve sharing things in common. In human friendships there are things we take on board to please our friends and things we leave behind so as not to offend them. So it is with our friendship with God. Companionship with him moulds us so that we become more and more like Christ. In our postmodern age it is depth of character – not image or professionalism – that people are looking for. So, if there's one thing I need to work on to be an effective Christian leader it is building a Christ-like character. I can only do that when I spend time with him.

Some may think that the principal of a Bible college has some advantages over those who have to work in 'the real world'. It would be foolish to pretend that wasn't so. I've also worked as a teacher and in an office, so I know the pressures of ordinary employment. But don't get too romantic a view of running a Bible college. My days are busy and full of unexpected interruptions. I have an organization to run, people to manage, finances to balance, regulations to keep and university authorities to satisfy. I know first-hand the pressures on people working in higher education these days. That's why I know that unless I meet with God before the start of the day I'm only going to be casually acquainted with him throughout the rest of it.

Sure to reach the destination

But, hey! This isn't about imposing a law. It's a delight to meet with God. And he loves me even when I fail. It's not all about the initiatives I take to meet with him. My life's journey so far surely proves that. He has taken so many initiatives in my life of which I was blissfully ignorant at the time. That's why my confidence is not in the way I practise any spiritual discipline, but in him alone. That explains why my favourite text is Philippians 1:6, 'being confident of this, that he who began a good work in you will carry it on to

completion until the day of Christ Jesus.' One day when I
ask the question, 'Are we there yet?' the answer will be a
resounding 'Yes!'. In the meantime, keep trusting.

Derek Tidball is the Principal of the
London School of Theology and
chair of the Evangelical Alliance
Council. He is a former president
of the Baptist Union and author of
some 20 books. Derek is married
to Dianne, who is also a Baptist
minister. They have one teenage
son, Richard, who is a Crusader.
Derek still manages to hold his own on a badminton
court against students (just!).

*Take a moment to reflect on what you have just read.
What one thing do you want to remember and apply in
your own journey?*

Write down a few notes for your 'faith travelogue' on the route you're following to reach your final destination and the company you're keeping along the way. Do you need to adjust your course at all?

Have You Got the Guts?

JON HANCOCK

Jon is excited about the journey ahead, and he takes time out from the CBBC studio to explain some of the reasons why.

Jon, as you reflect on your journey so far, what would you identify as some of the big life lessons God has been teaching you?

I can remember thinking over some pretty deep stuff when I was about twelve years old. That's not to say that I was a particularly deep thinking kind of kid but, for some reason, I just couldn't shake off thinking about certain things.

I didn't share this with anyone for many years – it was a very personal thing and I wouldn't have been able to describe what I was experiencing if someone had asked. I can distinctly remember lying in bed many nights and wondering about my life – and, more poignantly – my death. I was fraught with worry about how *long* eternity was! I daydreamed about how I could spend my time in heaven … learning to play football, maybe flying a kite for a bit (even for a few years) … but I'd still have eternity to fill. And this really bothered me. The more I thought about it, the more I descended down a spiral of anxiety, worry and fear. (I should point out that I never doubted for a moment that I would go to heaven – I'd always done the 'church thing' and heaven seemed a cert.)

I was troubled that I couldn't fit it all together. How could I allow myself to be governed by someone who made everything so big and scary? That question effectively prevented me from thinking of God as a loving Father with whom I could have a relationship. Everything about God felt too serious – much more for grown-ups than for kids. So I used to bargain with God – I'd have a really great life, then I'd come into a full relationship with him at about the same time I picked up my bus pass and pension book.

But I couldn't deny that in my mates, and in other young people at my church, there was real 'life'. They had energy and enthusiasm that I didn't have, and I was missing out. The lesson I learned is that God is for *now*. I guess I saw a bit of the true character of God. By putting

THE LESSON I LEARNED IS THAT GOD IS FOR *NOW*.

God off until another time I was depriving myself of an amazing relationship with someone who isn't a cosmic power force, but a caring and loving Creator. The fact that I didn't understand God wasn't really an excuse. If I *could* understand God he wouldn't be half as big as I thought he'd be. I don't understand how a car works, but I still get into one and travel places.

So I allowed God to take control, and he's led me to discover things and to jobs and relationships that I couldn't possibly have imagined or expected. It's been one heck of an adventure. Only he has the key to who I'm supposed to be and what I'm supposed to do. And, as for eternity, how can I be fearful of being with my Creator, the one who guides me and who I'm discovering more and more about every day of my life?

My life is not for wishing away – and God has a plan for me that I'm very excited about (I haven't got a clue what it is, but I'm still excited). One of my pastors used to say that the most important character on a tombstone is the dash: 22nd March 1904 – 14th June 1979. The dash will mark everything that my life has represented. I hope that's not the only mark I make on the world.

> *What aspect of the nature of God causes you to stand back and think, 'That's aweome!'?*

God's grace – I am so undeserving of what I have received.

There are times when I can kid myself that I was worth dying for ... and then there are times – true moments of haunting clarity – when I see just how dirty and sinful I am. And yet still he sent his Son.

I was once encouraged to write a letter to myself to remind me what God had taught me on a Christian youth event I was working at. Someone kept the letter sealed and safe and sent it back to me some months later. My letter read:

'God's grace is 100% him and 0% me. 'I can't even make it 1% me. It is undeserved and the only response is for me to give my all in my all. God's grace demands a reaction. Wow.'

GOD'S GRACE IS 100% HIM AND 0% ME.

> *Can you tell us how you're growing in intimacy with God? How do you connect with God in the midst of life's demands?*

I always feel slightly unnerved around people who announce with full certainty that they've heard God say something, or that they've discerned God's will. I meet some people who give the impression that God asks *them* for advice. But it's wrong for me to want to be intimate with God in a way that isn't right for me. I shouldn't have someone else's conversations with God – I need to have my own, and I shouldn't miss out on them.

In short, I'm growing in intimacy by doing things in faith (i.e., not really knowing whether they're right or not, but trusting that they are), pushing the barriers of things I know I can get better at. I mean that in a simple way. For example, I'm challenging myself to share what I feel God has told me in my prayers. It's sometimes difficult to make time to pray and even tougher to come away with something that I feel God has said to me. But I find it more difficult still to share what I feel God has said with other people. Sometimes I might feel that God might want me to encourage someone or lead them to a bit of the Bible, and I'm scared to think that I might be doing something wrong. But when it's right … wow, I really feel close – intimate – with God.

God has been helping me to grow recently in three different areas. When I first met my wife, she encouraged me to write my prayers down in a prayer diary and I've found this really helpful. Being an ordered, routine kind of guy, I love the action of writing something every day. But, more than that, I find that when I'm writing something down I'm not as easily distracted, so the time is more focused. Having this written record also allows me to look back on my prayers and think about what God has been showing me over months or years. I think hindsight is an amazing thing, and it's difficult to properly review what's happened if you're only relying on memory.

Second, I was challenged by a successful Christian businessman I met who told me about how he and a few friends (also successful Christian businessmen) have committed to phoning each other every week. Regardless of where they are in the world, no matter what time zone, they will phone to encourage and pray for each other. I have had prayer partners before, and I've found them helpful, but this commitment to accountability – irrespective of geography – inspired me. As a result, I now phone a great mate, Tim, and we speak each week to share and pray for one another. We have lots to learn about how best to use our time, but our conversation is built on a great love for and trust in one another, a strong passion for what God will do with each of us, and a commitment to make the partnership as fruitful as possible.

Third, I learn so much by seeing God through the Bible. Allowing his word to speak to me helps me to understand him. Rather than just reading the Bible (which I can treat as a 'read that bit – tick it off the list' activity), I try to sit down with a commentary and make notes of which bits – both in the Bible and in the commentary – jump out at me. It's been fantastic to feel excited by the Living Word and to know that the Holy Spirit has been doing business with me.

Can you tell us what your favourite passage in the Bible is and how you're applying it?

I love the Old Testament characters and have recently re-read and studied Gideon (Jgs. 6–8). I love his story first because he's such a normal guy. As far as he's concerned he's a nobody, but God uses him spectacularly. Yes, he has character issues, but God uses him nonetheless – that's encouraging.

I love dissecting how much of the story is God and how much is Gideon. God does some amazing things to prove to Gideon that he's there, but there's still a huge element of Gideon having to venture into the unknown. I believe God often requires blind faith – and like Gideon, I know enough about God's faithfulness to trust him, so there should be nothing stopping me.

There's the most amazing sense of God weaving events together to see his purposes through. God anticipates that Gideon will need more affirmation, so he sends a sign before Gideon has a chance to ask for one (Jgs. 7:9–15). God plants seeds of doubt in the minds of the enemy before Gideon has even attacked (Jgs. 7:13–14). And then God reduces Gideon's fighting force so dramatically that no one can doubt that it was God who won the battle.

In my life at the moment, I need to have that blind faith – to trust that I'm in the right place and that God is going ahead to shape events so that I will follow the path he has for me. It encourages me that God is for us and that he does not simply set us in motion and then sit back to watch which direction we go. I'm trying to grow as Gideon did – someone who becomes accustomed to God's leading and follows his call no matter how bizarre, dangerous or downright stupid what he says is.

Jon, what one piece of wisdom from your own journey would you like to share with your fellow travellers?

Don't walk your Christian journey alone. The power of friendship, loyalty, accountability and mutual help is staggering. Walking with others is a vulnerable activity, and it exposes us to the possibility of being hurt by people because we all make mistakes, but when it works it's a hugely rewarding thing. I believe we're all designed for teamwork, to work together, to make sense of God and complement each other's talents.

DON'T WALK YOUR CHRISTIAN JOURNEY ALONE.

When I walk stretches of my journey alone, my mind can play tricks on me – I can believe I'm being a much better follower of Christ than I am, and I can churn things over in my mind to the extent that I happily entertain unhelpful or damaging thoughts. When I'm not open or 'real' with others, I don't move forward in my relationship with God.

I work well with others. I enjoy the camaraderie and I benefit from being a help to – as well as being helped by – others. So I can honestly say that I'm proudest when I do or say something that is a blessing or godly challenge to friends that I love. Then I know God's using me. And I feel humble when I see how God has put the right people in the right places for me at just the right time. All I need to do is seek them out and allow myself to be blessed.

As you journey with God, please prayerfully consider whether there is someone who knows where you are at with God. Is there someone who can challenge you in your relationship with God and help you in the work you're doing? It doesn't have to be someone who is in your existing group of friends or someone your age or with similar experiences – it might be someone whose faith you've admired for a while, someone who you know is more experienced with God than you are. Our family members in Christ have such a depth of experience, love, support and prayers available. The Bible is full of examples of people gaining strength from working together, and I believe that opening ourselves to other people for moulding and encouragement is something God smiles upon. Don't journey alone.

Jon is married to Ems. They have one son, Sam, and identical twin boys on the way! He has worked for CBBC since 2000 and is currently a studio director.

Take a moment to reflect on what you have just read. What one thing do you want to remember and apply in your own journey?

Why do you think it takes guts to complete the Christian journey?

Do Not Worry

JENNY BAKER

Jenny, a writer and presenter for Damaris, shares some key life lessons as she reflects on God's provision and care throughout the seasons of her journey so far.

Jenny, as you reflect on your journey so far, what would you identify as some of the big life lessons God has been teaching you?

One of the key lessons that God has taught me has been to trust him for his provision. When Jonny and I got married we had Matthew 6:19–34 read at our wedding – a passage that I have returned to again and again. 'Do not store up for yourselves treasure on earth ... You cannot serve both God and Money ... do not worry about your life, what you will eat or drink ... seek first his kingdom and his righteousness, and all these things will be given to you as well.' We decided not to buy a house when we got married, but rather to rent so that we weren't tied down with a big mortgage and were free to work for Youth for Christ. Although family and friends advised us to get on the housing ladder, we decided that we would trust God to provide housing for us – and he has ever since, firstly in Bath and more recently in London.

In 1995, we felt God prompting us to move to London. We knew that we would never be able to afford to buy a house in London, and so we would have to continue renting. But how do you decide where to live in such a huge city? We had two children by that stage and needed to find a school for Joel, as well as the right environment for them to grow up in. 'Do not worry about your life ... seek first the kingdom.' We prayed hard, came up to London and spent a week looking around but just felt bewildered. Two months before we needed to move, we had a letter from friends saying, 'Have you thought of living in Ealing? There are good schools there.' After receiving this letter I went to a day conference in London and met someone who knew a vicar whose curate was moving out. That same day, my dad sent us a newspaper cutting featuring that same curate with a note that said, 'Maybe you could live in his house.' And, yes, he lived in Ealing.

We contacted Douglas Holt, the vicar, and he invited us to lunch the next Sunday. We saw the house and loved it and found out about local schools. I rang the school on Monday to be told they had a waiting list of 70 pupils, but on Thursday they rang back to say we could have a place 'if you really go to church'.

The way everything slotted into place just at the right time was fantastic – although I confess that I did worry about what was going to happen to us. I told myself that, next time we had to move, I would trust God and not worry. We have been very happy in Ealing. One of the best things has been getting involved in 'Grace', an alternative worship service at St Mary's Ealing, and being part of its development. Our boys are very settled and happy in schools with some good friends. So, in 2001 when the church needed the house back and we had to move out, we wanted to stay in the area. House prices, both for rental and purchase, had shot up again, and we needed another small miracle of God's provision.

We came up with a creative way of buying a house – we would try to get people to invest in the house with us, lend us money for ten years and share in the profits when the house is sold at the end of that time. Again it was an anxious time, and I reread that passage in Matthew many times. 'Your heavenly Father knows what you need.' To cut a long story short, we set ourselves a deadline to raise the money and, on that day, we had just enough to buy the one house in our price range that we liked. That was a few years ago, and it has been a brilliant move. It's been great to be able to buy our own house, but in a few years we will need to pay back our generous investors and so may well find ourselves in the same position again – needing to find somewhere to live with very little money. Part of me would love the security of a big salary and a house that was all my own; but another part of me is very glad that I need to continue to rely on God to provide for me. In a few years we'll be on another adventure of faith, needing God to provide for us. So I'll be back to Matthew again.

The second key lesson that I have had to learn is that God has given me gifts that he wants me to use. That may sound like a very obvious thing to say, but I've had to battle with two things. Firstly, I was brought up in the Brethren church where women were not allowed to speak in public meetings, to hold positions of leadership, to have any kind of authority or to teach. One of my earliest memories of church is of a woman standing up in the morning service and reading from the Bible. About ten people stormed out in protest. While I was at university and wrestling with making my faith my own, this was a real sticking point for me. I hated the fact that the faith I had been brought up in put me down as a woman, but I couldn't quite turn my back on the God who had been with me all my life.

In my final year at university, I joined a church where there were lots of people who really wanted to think through the Christian faith and how it related to all areas of life. I joined a study group which looked at all of the Bible's teaching on the roles of men and women and my eyes were opened to a different way of understanding the passages that had been so painful to read before. Instead of the church oppressing women, I saw that the gospel actually liberates all of us, men and women, to reach our true potential in Christ. I've been blessed with a husband who shares the same theology of men and women and who has given me the push I've needed at times to take on things even when I've felt inadequate. We see our marriage very much as a partnership of equals, and we try to enable each other to develop our gifts and grow as people. When our children were little, we job-shared, working half a week each and spending the other half with the boys. At one time, I directed Bath YFC and was technically Jonny's boss; now his work takes more time than mine, but we still aim to share work, housework and parenting so that we can both follow our other callings as well.

Understanding the issue of biblical equality in my head was one thing; believing it in my heart was another and it has been an uphill battle against low self-esteem and self-hatred to accept that God really does love me and has given me gifts that he wants to use in his kingdom. For many years I have struggled with feelings of self-doubt and worthlessness. Anyone who has gone through something similar will know that no

> I REALIZED THAT I HAD A CHOICE – TO BELIEVE WHAT GOD SAID ABOUT ME, OR TO BELIEVE WHAT I FELT INSIDE.

matter what your achievements, if the voice inside you says you are useless, then that's how you feel. A few years ago I experienced something of a turning point when I was reading Ephesians 1 about being chosen and loved by God. I realized that I had a choice – to believe what God said about me, or to believe what I felt inside. I decided that what God said was true and I have tried to use his word, often through gritted teeth, to drown out the internal chorus of 'You're useless, stupid, worthless' and so on. That has been helpful, but I wouldn't say I'm completely there yet. I still need to have my view of myself transformed into the way God sees me.

> *What aspect of the nature of God causes you to stand back and think, 'That's awesome!'?*

The thing that most amazes me about God is his faithfulness to me, in spite of my faults and failings. Only I know fully the mistakes that I keep making and my stubbornness – but God is always willing to forgive me and show his love to me again and again. In supplying us with our housing, through my family, in providing me with work over the four years I've been self-employed, God has proved his faithfulness. I want to make sure I stay in the place where I need God to be faithful to me; I don't want to get too comfortable or too confident in my own ability.

I WANT TO MAKE SURE I STAY IN THE PLACE WHERE I NEED GOD TO BE FAITHFUL TO ME; I DON'T WANT TO GET TOO COMFORTABLE OR TOO CONFIDENT IN MY OWN ABILITY.

> *Can you tell us how you're growing in intimacy with*
> *God? How do you connect with God in the midst of life's*
> *demands?*

I have always struggled with having a regular time to read
my Bible and pray. I grew up with the tyranny of the Quiet
Time hanging over me. I have kept a journal intermittently
over the years and the most common entry has to be 'I
must read my Bible and pray more.' I don't write that
any more – not because I don't need to or because I've
changed my ways, but because the truth of our intentions
is revealed in our actions, not our words. I just need to get
on and do it.

Three things have helped me grow in intimacy with
God over the last few years.

One is the work that I do. Writing materials for Christian
organizations means that I regularly need to read the Bible
just to do my work. Recently, for example, I wrote six
hundred notes to be inserted into the text of a new youth
Bible. To do that I had to read the whole Bible, looking for
interesting things to insert evenly throughout the 66 books.
It was a fantastic way to get an overview of the Bible and
to be reminded of some of the great themes in salvation
history. I used to feel guilty that it was often only work
that made me turn to the Bible, but I think I now have a
less dualistic view. God is in my work, after all.

Secondly, the style of worship at Grace really fits
me – it's interactive, reflective, participative. You can't
sit back and be a spectator or get lost in a crowd. The
worship draws people into an encounter with God that's
personal.

And, thirdly, I've been exploring a more contemplative
style of praying, sitting in God's presence and listening to

him instead of coming with a long list of requests. Simon Barrington Ward came to Grace last January and talked about the Jesus Prayer – 'Lord Jesus Christ, Son of God, have mercy on me'. I made myself a prayer cord and for about eight months prayed the Jesus Prayer a hundred times every morning. It maybe sounds mechanistic, but I found it a really helpful way of praying that enabled me to engage with God. More recently I have got out of the habit of doing it so regularly, but I still return to this way of praying when I know I need to be still in God's presence. I think I have learned to be much more relaxed in my relationship with God – to know that I don't need to impress him or try to be something that I'm not. God accepts and loves me as I am. Having said that, I know that I do need to make more space in my life at the moment to grow in intimacy with God.

Jenny, what one piece of wisdom from your own journey would you like to share with your fellow travellers?

The piece of wisdom that has most helped me in my journey of faith, and which I'd like to pass on to others, came from Carol Henderson at Greenbelt nearly 17 years ago. I remember sitting in her caravan backstage feeling very vulnerable and fragile because I felt so far from God, but I was unable to put any of that into words or ask for the help that I needed. She said that in our spiritual lives we go through seasons. Sometimes it will feel like summer, when it's warm and wonderful and everything is growing. At other times we will go through a period of autumn when it feels like everything is dying and we are losing the

BUT SPRING ALWAYS COMES, AND WITH IT SIGNS OF NEW LIFE AND THE PROMISE OF GROWTH.

intimacy that we thought we had. Then sometimes we will go through a spell of winter, when there is no sign of life and God feels far away. But spring always comes, and with it signs of new life and the promise of growth. That helped me understand what I was going through at that time and has proved to be invaluable wisdom time and again.

Jenny Baker was a teacher and a youth worker for many years. She is now a freelance writer and presents the President for a Day experience for Damaris in schools. She is the author of *Tune In, Chill Out* (Birmingham: Christian Education, 2004) – about using contemplative prayer in youth work. She is a Greenbelt trustee.

Take a moment to reflect on what you have just read. What one thing do you want to remember and apply in your own journey?

***What is worrying you now? How can you trust God with
this – whatever it may be?***

Make it Happen

MATT BIRD

Matt is the founder of a public affairs company called 'Make it Happen' (because people say that's what he does!). Here he shares a bit about how God has been making it happen in his journey so far ...

Matt, as you reflect on your journey so far, what would you identify as some of the big life lessons God has been teaching you?

There is nothing worse than a 'know-it-all Christian' – and I should know, as I used to be one. I thought that maturing in my relationship with God meant knowing more 'biblical answers' to life's dilemmas. I used to pride myself in how well I knew the Bible and in my thought-through responses to the challenges of life.

However, one of the big lessons that I have learned through my life experience so far is that 'crap happens'. There is no apparent reason why. Sometimes bad stuff happens to good people, and good stuff happens to bad people. As followers of Jesus Christ we are not immunized from harm. But we can be sure that God is with us, and sustaining us, through the great adventure of life.

I have discovered that life in relationship with God is about faith, and not certainty. Often, when we first surrender our lives to God, we think that we have discovered all the answers to life.

I HAVE DISCOVERED THAT LIFE IN RELATIONSHIP WITH GOD IS ABOUT FAITH, AND NOT CERTAINTY.

Only through the years do we discover that we have seen a few promises fulfilled but continue to live with much uncertainty. Wondering at the mystery of God is much more a hallmark of being a mature follower than fooling ourselves, and others, that we 'know it all'.

> *What aspect of the nature of God causes you to stand back and think, 'That's awesome!'?*

Self-constraint! Wow! The fact that God provides guidelines for living and then gives us complete freedom shows incredible self-constraint on his part.

The picture that best illustrates God's self-constraint and our freedom is that of the Garden of Eden. God created the universe and then created man and woman and placed them in a garden in which they had complete freedom to eat from any tree they chose – except one. God did not put them in creation and say, 'There is only one tree you can eat from, and only one choice in life'.

Basically I am saying that there is a massive myth about guidance. We are not walking God's 'tightrope' of obedience so that, unless we comply, disaster will strike us. No, God liberates us to enjoy

IF WE LOVE GOD, WE CAN DO WHAT WE LIKE.

the great adventure called life in all its fullness with him. If we love God, we can do what we like.

> *Can you tell us how you're growing in intimacy with God? How do you connect with God in the midst of life's demands?*

Strangely, I often feel distant from God in set piece, or more traditional services with singing, listening to the preacher and so on – regardless of their style. I actually connect most with God in other ways.

One of my favourite ways of doing this is sitting in my club chair listening to classical music, especially anything by John Rutter. I find there is something deeply 'other' about the creativity and power of music.

Whenever time allows, I enjoy reading – particularly biographies of people who have made a difference with their lives. It's inspiring to see how others have survived the highs and lows of life, and they inspire me with hope.

Walking and water do it for me. I enjoy a good stroll, and particularly close to the sea or a river, lake or pond. Though it is hard to explain, there is something both peaceful and powerful about water.

I find love, acceptance and honesty sitting around a table eating and drinking (and occasionally praying) with friends. I think we need a revival of feasting – God's people were big into it in the Old Testament and Jesus did a lot of it – it's time to get it going again.

Talk about intimacy with God can often become a human-focused endeavour rather than simply finding a place, person or activity that allows a person to find peace with God.

> *What's your favourite passage in the Bible, and how are you applying it?*

One of my favourite biblical stories is that of Joseph in Genesis 37–50.

Joseph was favoured by God and framed by people. In his household he was favoured by his father and framed by his brothers. As a slave he was favoured by Potiphar and framed by his wife. In prison he was favoured by the guards and framed by his fellow prisoners. He never became cynical about God, or about people. He simply tried to live for, and serve God wherever he was and whatever he was doing. That is my aspiration.

Another reason I love Joseph is because he was a leader who worked out his faith in the mainstream of society. He was not a priest or a prophet, he was a politician. In fact, he became prime minister of Egypt. He integrated his faith and public life, and that is also something I aspire to.

The greatest theological cancer in the church today is the sacred-secular divide. It is this idea that being with God's people in congregation is sacred and enables us to be

THE GREATEST THEOLOGICAL CANCER IN THE CHURCH TODAY IS THE SACRED-SECULAR DIVIDE.

closest and most obedient to him; whereas when we are in the world we are most distant from God and most likely to be disobedient to him. This thinking and mindset immunize the impact of the church in God's world.

Rather, I believe like the psalmist that the earth is the Lord's and everything in it (Ps. 24:1), and the world is the object of God's love to redeem and not condemn (Jn. 3:16–17). God's mission is to restore the whole created order, and his people are never going to do that in a ghetto but only as journalists, business leaders, doctors, teachers, retailers and politicians like Joseph.

> *Matt, what one piece of wisdom from your own journey would you like to share with your fellow travellers?*

Believe in 'original goodness' more than 'original sin'. Now hear me out ... I am *not* saying that original sin does not exist; we only have to look at the shortcomings in our own lives and in society to see that things are not quite as God meant them to be. But the divine order and biblical emphasis show us that goodness precedes sin.

For example, Genesis talks about creation being 'very good' before it talks about corruption. In the New Testament, it is clear that Jesus always saw goodness in people before he saw their sin – whether in the woman caught in adultery or in Zacchaeus the tax collector or in Thomas the disciple full of doubt. The one exception to this would be the religious people who thought they had no sin.

Our church traditions have emphasized the doctrine of original sin at the expense of original goodness. This perhaps explains why it is easier for 'Christians' to be known for what we are against rather than what we are for.

Schooling and education have changed so much over recent years. The approach of 'positive behaviour management', identifying good behaviour in even the most naughty children, draws out more good behaviour. In the past naughty children were chastised, which only led to more bad behaviour. Perhaps education is learning to believe in 'original goodness' more than in 'original sin', and so should we in our households, neighbourhoods, friendships, workplaces and congregations.

Matt is married to Esther and they have a son, Joseph. They live in Wimbledon, where Matt is a councillor in local government and enjoys playing racquet sports (matt bird@makeithappenuk.com).

Take a moment to reflect on what you have just read. What one thing do you want to remember and apply in your own journey?

What do you want God to 'make happen' in your spiritual growth?

Freedom in Christ

SHARON PRIOR

If you've ever had any doubts about the sufficiency of God's word for conversion, your self-image, or different ways to worship and serve God, Sharon's journey so far will connect with yours ...

> *Sharon, as you reflect on your journey so far, what would you identify as some of the big life lessons God has been teaching you?*

I have been a Christian now for over 20 years, and I am amazed at how much God has taught me – but Christians never stop learning. We have probably all had the experience of God teaching us something new from a Bible passage that we thought we knew well. A few of the big lessons that God has been teaching me (and continues to remind me of) concern knowing myself through knowing God and using the gifts he gives.

First, I have learned that it is only when I know God and understand my position in Christ that I can truly know who I am. Many people struggle with self-image, and we are told that it is a big area of concern for young people in particular. Many years ago I read a book by Josh McDowell called *His Image, My Image*[1] that helped me to grasp this concept. Ephesians 1 and 2 clearly explain our position in Christ. We need to understand this fundamental truth for ourselves and communicate it to others, and perhaps especially to young people in our care.

Secondly, I have learned the importance of getting on with the job of using the gifts that God has given us rather than wanting other people's gifts. Often when we are jealous of other people's gifts we miss out on the gifts that God has given us. I had not been a Christian long when some friends formed a drama group. I wanted to be part of the group, but I have never been very good at drama and actually don't really enjoy it. But I saw the impact that these friends had as people responded to the gospel through their drama, and I wanted to be part of that. It took a wise person to point out to me that drama was not a gift that God had given me and I was wasting time, because desiring another person's gift meant that I was not using the gifts that he had given me. We all need to identify the gifts God has given us and get on and use them. 1 Peter 4:10 encourages us to do this: 'Each one should use whatever gift he has received to serve others.'

> OFTEN WHEN WE ARE JEALOUS OF OTHER PEOPLE'S GIFTS WE MISS OUT ON THE GIFTS THAT GOD HAS GIVEN US.

What aspect of the nature of God causes you to stand back and think, 'That's awesome!'?

There are many things about God that fill me with awe. The Isle of Purbeck is my favourite place in this country. I have been involved in many Crusader camps at Studland and seen God move in the lives of young people and adults alike. When I stand on that Crusader campsite and think of the history (Crusaders have been camping there for over 70 years), of how many people have decided to follow Jesus here, it makes me stand back in awe.

However, I think the most amazing thing about God is that he reaches out and speaks into people's lives even when they are not looking for him. I became a Christian at the age of twenty-one. I had no contact with church or with Christians, but my brother had been given a Gideon New Testament when he was ten years old and it had been in a box in our loft, unread, for 11 years. I started to read from the beginning and, when I got to the story of Nicodemus in John 3, I realized that there was something missing in my life and I needed to ask Jesus to help me. I got on my knees beside my bed that day and have not looked back since. I learned several important lessons from this experience.

First and foremost, God is faithful. I do not know who gave the Gideon New Testament to my brother all those years previously, and that person will never know the impact this gift has had on my life. But God is faithful to his promises, and 'so is my word that goes out from my mouth: It will not return to me empty, but will accomplish what I desire and achieve the purpose for which I sent it' (Isa. 55:11). The Gideon who went into my brother's school was being faithful to what God had called him to do. We need to be faithful in all of our work for God – even if we do not see the outcomes.

FIRST AND FOREMOST, GOD IS FAITHFUL.

Second, I learned through my conversion experience that God's word is powerful. I did not know any Christians when I made a decision to follow Jesus; nobody explained the gospel to me. I was convicted through God's word. We need to realize that the Bible is a living word and that it is powerful. Sometimes we need to let it speak for itself and never be cautious of using it to speak truth into people's lives. It is also important that we pray

WE NEED TO REALIZE THAT THE BIBLE IS A LIVING WORD AND THAT IT IS POWERFUL.

that God's Holy Spirit will work in people's hearts so they can understand what God is saying to them through his word.

> *Can you tell us how you're growing in intimacy with God? How do you connect with God in the midst of life's demands?*

You only have to walk into a Christian bookshop and you fall over books on how to be intimate with God. As a young Christian I read many of these books, however they never seemed to have the required effect. I was taught that it is very important to have a daily Quiet Time, and I have to say that it is an area that I have struggled with throughout my Christian life.

About a year ago a friend recommended a book called *Sacred Pathways* by Gary Thomas. This book really has helped me in my relationship with God. It points out that when we talk about being intimate with God we tend to think that one size fits all – and, from my experience and that of many of my friends, that is clearly not true. I have been in lively praise times that have done nothing for my relationship with God, while others seem to have grown much closer to God through them. I'm afraid that I find singing the same songs over and over again boring and irrelevant to my walk with God. In the past this has made me feel unspiritual, and I have felt condemned by other Christians who cannot understand this.

When we look at God's word we see many different characters who all related to God in different ways:

> Abraham had a religious bent and built altars everywhere he went. Moses and Elijah revealed an activist's streak in their various confrontations with forces of evil and in their conversations with God. David celebrated God with an enthusiastic style of worship, while his son, Solomon, expressed his love for God by offering generous sacrifices. Ezekiel and John described loud and colourful images of God. Mordecai demonstrated his love for God by caring for others. Mary sat at Jesus' feet in contemplation.[2]

Through this book I have found the pathways that help me to connect with God and to worship God in a way that suits my personality. I have since felt liberated in my walk with God, which has helped me in my work with young people as I talk about how they can relate to God more effectively.

The times when I feel most engaged with God are when I get out in the open air and walk in the forest or on the cliff top. At these times it's almost as if God is walking with me and I can talk with him and tell him how much I love him. Gary Thomas says: 'Walks that are truly helpful are walks in which I lay down my agenda at the first sign of grass and let God lead my mind where he may.'[3] I am not always on my own – sometimes I walk with friends and together we explore what God is saying and lift our voices in praise and worship. Other friends struggle to understand this, as they feel closer to God in a worship service.

Serving others is another way that I worship God. Working in a team to achieve a task that will benefit someone else helps me to feel closer to God. As Thomas says, 'Attending to "spiritual concerns" is not an excuse for refusing to get our hands dirty.'[4] All of this does not mean that God doesn't speak to me in church through a song or the sermon, but this book helped me to see that I am not less spiritual because I feel closer to God when I am outdoors or serving others.

> *What's your favourite passage in the Bible, and how are you applying it?*

There are many passages that I could choose from, but if I had to choose one it would have to be Ephesians 1 and 2. This passage talks about the abundance of God – the writer uses words like 'every spiritual blessing' and 'lavished'. This is not a God who holds back, but one who gives freely. As I said, this helps me to understand my position in Christ and the resources I have available to me as a Christian. When things go wrong in my work or I make a mistake in a leadership decision I need to be reminded that I am not a bad person or a failure. A friend once said to me that Christians should be the very people who realize that failure is not final. But so often we don't understand this, and we feel condemned by something we have done wrong or a bad decision we have made. As a leader I also have to take criticism and negative feedback – it comes with the territory. No one can please everybody all of the time. It is so easy to take the criticism and not assess it objectively. It is so easy to let it affect the way we do things in the future, rather than learning lessons from it and moving on.

There are times when I need to be reminded that I am 'blessed ... with every spiritual blessing in Christ' (Eph. 1:3), that I am 'chosen' (Eph. 1:11) and that I was 'included in Christ when I heard the word of truth' (Eph. 1:13). When I worked at Moorlands College I often asked the students to read through Ephesians 1 and list all the things that it says about who they are in Christ. I then encouraged them

ANY UNWISE DECISION
OR MISTAKE YOU MAKE
CANNOT CHANGE YOUR
POSITION IN CHRIST.

to write this list on a piece of paper and put it above their computer or on the fridge at home, so that they were constantly being reminded of what it means to be 'in Christ'.

I would encourage you to do this and see how it can affect your attitude to failure. Any unwise decision or mistake you make cannot change your position in Christ.

> *Sharon, what one piece of wisdom from your own journey would you like to share with your fellow travellers?*

Many years ago a friend of mine had a carved wooden plaque on the wall in his house, which you could see as soon as you walked through the front door. It said, 'Beware of the barrenness of a busy life'. This saying has been with me ever since. I have tended to try and earn God's love by doing lots of things, but I can never earn God's love. Nothing I do will make God love me more and nothing I do or do not do will make him love me less. This has been a hard lesson to learn.

Youth work is a never-ending job. Building relationships with young people takes time, and leaders need to be there for the long haul. I can get so caught up with serving that I don't see the one I am serving, and my relationship with God suffers. So my advice would be to make sure that you are not so busy that you do not have time to invest in your own spiritual growth. Gary Thomas says that we need to be careful to make sure that we 'tend the garden of the soul.'[5] He says, 'I want to faithfully serve God for fifty or sixty or seventy years, which means I need to consider how I can be spiritually replenished.'[6]

Think through how you can continually be transformed spiritually in your life. Don't delay!

Sharon Prior is head of voluntary ministry at Scripture Union, where she develops strategies for recruiting more volunteers and identifying their training needs. Previously she worked at Moorlands College as a lecturer, where she was responsible for the degree course in Community and Family Studies. She has also been a volunteer with Crusaders for many years.

Take a moment to reflect on what you have just read. What one thing do you want to remember and apply in your own journey?

How can your life reflect the freedom of Christ more deeply, knowing that nothing you do, good or bad, can change your position in Christ?

Servanthood = Greatness

STEPHEN RILEY

YFC worker and founding member of Dependance, Stephen has been learning a lot about balance, accountability and service ...

Stephen, as you reflect on your journey so far, what would you identify as some of the big life lessons God has been teaching you?

God has been teaching me three lessons in particular: first, that relationship is key to ministry; second, that openness is key to discipleship; and third, that rhythm and routine don't stifle us but rather set us free. Allow me to explain.

No matter how talented or eloquent I am in the ministry God has given me; no matter how well I know the Bible and am able to explain it to others; no matter how many young people I lead towards the love of Christ, if my relationships with my wife, children, church family, work family and friends and neighbours aren't good, then I can't expect to bear fruit. It's a simple principle that sometimes I tend to avoid. Confronting people, loving others the way they need to be loved, serving others and so on are all just as important as me standing on a stage and rapping or preaching my heart out.

Second, I must make myself vulnerable to God in everything. That sometimes means being open with others when I don't want to be. There is the fear of being vulnerable and not wanting to always come into the light. The Bible says,

SECOND, I MUST MAKE MYSELF VULNERABLE TO GOD IN EVERYTHING.

'above all else guard your heart for it is the wellspring of life' (Prov. 4:23). Surely you can't just be open with anybody about anything? Well, I find that having people besides my wife who will ask me the questions that spur me on, those questions that challenge my behaviour and my supposedly well-thought-out strategies, is enough to keep me on the straight and narrow. Some call it accountability. Christians need to be honest and model what it means to live for Jesus – otherwise it is all just hypocrisy, which Jesus slammed the Pharisees for.

Third, if I practise rhythm with my routine, then it actually creates space for me to become more intimate with God, and with my family and friends, and they will trust me more because they'll know I have allocated that time to them. Rhythm with my routine means trying to organize my life instead of doing things in random bits and pieces whenever it suits me. I have tried, for example, to shut off work at five o'clock and give time to other people or things that are not work related. I'm an extrovert; I love to fill time and space. I love to talk and dance, and anything else energetic, but even people like me need space to recharge. I need to do things that are completely unrelated to my work, things that bring me great joy – going to the gym, doing gymnastics, watching my son play footie, taking my daughter out. If I don't carve out time for these things on a regular basis, then it's not long before I get frustrated.

> What aspect of the nature of God causes you to stand back
> and think, 'That's awesome!'?

There are many, but the greatest of all has to be grace. The
Bible says that, from the fullness of his grace, we have
all received one blessing after another. I know we aren't
supposed to add to the Bible, but if I were inspired back
then I would have continued to write '... even when we
don't deserve it'.

In his book *What's so Amazing about Grace?* Philip Yancey
writes, 'Grace is Christianity's best gift to the world, a
spiritual nova in our midst exerting a force stronger
than vengeance.'[7] And it's true. The most amazing thing
about grace is that grace is amazing. In his book *The Grace
Awakening*, Charles Swindoll talks about grace killers.[8]
These are people who would rather live pharisaic lives to
the letter of the law than depend on and live out the grace
of God in their lives.

I believe that every person wants to hear routinely
the same words that Jesus spoke to the woman caught
in the act of adultery. *'Neither do I condemn you.'* I know
from my own Christian background that whenever I got
things wrong it wasn't always grace that I experienced.
Sometimes it was guilt ... and the two are so far apart.

Watching *The Passion* brought back to me the reality
of the grace of God in my life. Throughout the film I was
thanking God because of what Jesus did. Imagine if God
had made the punishment that Jesus took in our place our
National Service. How many of us could have taken that
first punch without saying anything, without pleading
for our rights, without calling out to God to make it stop?
When the film was over, the friend I took with me who isn't
a Christian (yet) clearly didn't see the personal application
of it – and I think I was more gob-smacked by that than

by what I had seen minutes before. I realized that grace is completely alien to unbelievers and nearly impossible for them to see. Unless they see it fleshed out by Christians at large, then even such an excellent film portrayal could bypass them. My friend's reaction reminded me how I need to continually show him the grace of Jesus. I can do that by listening to him.

Grace is my motivator to not sin. Grace is my motivator to liberate others (and young people especially) from some of the 'to do lists' that we think help us to be disciples. Grace brings us back to the authentic gospel, no strings attached.

GRACE IS MY MOTIVATOR TO NOT SIN.

Can you tell us how you're growing in intimacy with God? How do you connect with God in the midst of life's demands?

You know, I don't even know. The obvious thing would be to talk about my daily devotional times with the Lord. I don't know if I'm regular in anything apart from cleaning my teeth. I'm not even sure if regularity brings intimacy. I heard Oral Roberts' wife say on TV the other day: 'I have to have the presence of God.' I go along with that. My everlasting prayer is that God would continually make me aware of his presence, for the more conscious I am of him, the more it will affect my conscience – what I think and how I think.

It's harder to sin when you're aware of him close by. The Lord is with me and he loves me. Now I know there are people reading this who are wondering how I get away with that. Sure, we all need discipline and routine, but I also believe that God needs to invade my routine. There is a danger that I become self-righteous in my routine, thinking that just because I read the Bible or pray at certain times each day I am becoming more intimate with God and doing the right thing. Spending time with God is a necessity. It is good to let God know that he has your attention at particular times in a day. We must be careful not to deceive ourselves by thinking that just because we've given him that part then he doesn't or can't have any other part. We need to be open to him 24/7.

> ON THE WHOLE, MY GROWTH IN INTIMACY COMES WHEN I ALLOW GOD TO BE GOD IN MY LIFE AND I DON'T SEEK TO TAKE THAT ROLE MYSELF.

On the whole, my growth in intimacy comes when I allow God to be God in my life and I don't seek to take that role myself.

What's your favourite passage in the Bible, and how are you applying it?

I have many favourite passages in the Bible, but I think the one that stands out above them all is James 1, where the author talks to Christians about a mature life being one of perseverance.

When I became a Christian I started to learn the book of James by heart. I got a little way into chapter 4 and then stopped. Did I really understand what I was reading? Whenever I have hit rock-bottom times in my life, regardless of the cause, the words of James 1 have come to my mind like a missile.

> Consider it pure joy, my brothers, whenever you face trials of many kinds, because you know that the testing of your faith develops perseverance. (v. 3)

(By the way, a trial is a happening that is happening in your life that isn't happening the way you want it to happen.)

Then later he says, 'Blessed is the man who perseveres under trial, because when he has stood the test, he will receive the crown of life that God has promised to those who love him' (v. 12). These are the 'spurring-on' verses in Scripture for me. When I trained as a youth worker in Youth for Christ, we were encouraged to look for those life verses – the ones that would keep us steadfast when we doubted our calling or were facing trials in our lives.

Stephen, what one piece of wisdom from your own journey would you like to share with your fellow travellers?

Servanthood is not a stepping-stone to greatness; it is greatness.

> SERVANTHOOD IS NOT
> A STEPPING-STONE
> TO GREATNESS; IT IS
> GREATNESS.

Everybody wants to be great, or to do something great. We want to be remembered for our greatness; we don't want to feel like we didn't do much with our lives. In my job, I get the opportunity to speak to thousands of young people, but on a one-to-one level is where the greatness is. Serving is awesome. It's an opportunity to take our eyes off ourselves and bless others

As a platform performer, I find it hard to serve in small ways. Bizarre isn't it, when the pinnacle of my Christian faith is servanthood? The challenge to the performer is to do those things that won't be seen, that won't be recognized by others because if it's not visual it's not obvious. Even when I do those things that won't be seen, the challenge is then to not feel like I need to tell everyone about it.

The way we view the people we serve often determines our attitude towards servanthood. Serving other people (wherever we are) is the greatest thing we can do because it is a testimony to the great things God has done in our lives.

 Stephen Riley works for Youth for Christ North East and is the director of Dependance, a rap dance and theatre company. Dependance spend 80% of their time in schools presenting the gospel to teenagers in ways that are accessible to them. Stephen is married with three children but has no pets (he doesn't like cats and finds dog too noisy). As well as being involved in various events throughout the year like Harvest Summer camp, Spring Harvest and IXth hour, his hobbies are playing guitar, chilling with the children and discussing with his wife. She tends to keep him sane.

Take a moment to reflect on what you have just read.
What one thing do you want to remember and apply in
your own journey?

How do you serve God and others in small ways that
aren't seen?

Taste and See that the Lord is Good

STEVE UPPAL

Steve began his journey with God at a young age. Here he reflects on how God has been challenging and sustaining him through many changes and seasons ...

I have been walking with Jesus for 25 years, since the age of five, and have been involved in Christian ministry for about 17 years. When I was a teenager, I led a group of friends who felt challenged to take the 'uncompromised gospel' to others. We called ourselves 'Christian Warriors' and used drama, mime, song, rap, multimedia and the spoken word to present the gospel. We travelled around the UK to youth meetings, schools, prisons, university Christian Union groups and churches, and we also did open-air presentations and evangelism training.

In 2001 I transitioned out of itinerant work into pastoring a church. I knew the change was coming for a number of years – it was a matter of waiting for the right timing. In addition to pastoring a local church I am involved in missions work in a number of countries and still have a passion for youth work.

> Trust in the LORD with all your heart and lean not on your own understanding; in all your ways

acknowledge him, and he will make your paths straight. (Prov. 3:5–6)

> *Steve, as you reflect on your journey so far, what would you identify as some of the big life lessons God has been teaching you?*

One of the hardest lessons I have had to learn is to trust. I like to do things myself and am always figuring things out, sorting situations and planning for the future. While it is good for us to work hard and do what we can, the danger is that we begin to look to our own ability (or inability) rather than trusting and acknowledging God. I have learned to trust that God is in control and to look to him to do what I cannot do. Living this way brings peace. God has called me, therefore he will sustain me and complete in me that which he has begun (Phil. 1:6). A big part of trusting God is acknowledging him in all we do and learning to submit things to him and to ask for help. I have learned to talk to him about everything and ask for his help, wisdom and grace.

Working with people is challenging and sometimes difficult. I have often wanted to see change come in people's lives far more quickly than it does. Part of trusting God, too, is believing that seed sown in people's lives will bear fruit in due season – even if I don't see change immediately. I have learned to commit people to God rather than get stressed and work things out in my own understanding.

I HAVE LEARNED TO COMMIT PEOPLE TO GOD RATHER THAN GET STRESSED AND WORK THINGS OUT IN MY OWN UNDERSTANDING.

I have also had to guard my heart against scepticism and cynicism, because it is very easy for us to become sceptical and cynical in our attitudes towards people. I need to trust people – they are not the enemy, but good. I need God's grace to stay tender, trusting and to believe the best about people. I have been hurt and mistreated by people, but I have made up my mind that I will keep trusting, giving and believing the best about people – no matter what happens.

What aspect of the nature of God causes you to stand back and think, 'That's awesome!'?

The one characteristic of God that has been very real and life changing for me is his goodness.

> Taste and see that the LORD is good; blessed is the man who takes refuge in him. (Ps. 34:8)

God is good – I believe it now.

When I was growing up I believed that God was all powerful, all knowing, ever present – but I wasn't sure if he was pleased with me. I felt like I had to try to impress him, make him like me or win his favour. For years I rode a roller coaster of feelings controlled by whether or not I felt I had pleased God. Had I prayed enough? Read enough? Fasted enough? Had I watched too much television? Depending on how I felt I had performed, I would feel good or bad – which in turn affected my day, my week, or an even longer period of time. Then I heard someone speak who said, 'your acceptance with God is not based on your performance but on Christ's performance on the cross.' As I realized that I was accepted and loved by God because of the work of the cross of Christ, I began a journey of freedom. I have a simple theology: God good, devil bad, and God is for

THIS MAY SOUND BASIC, BUT SO MANY CHRISTIANS DOUBT THE GOODNESS OF GOD. THEY THINK HE IS ANGRY OR UPSET WITH THEM.

me. I believe God loves me, accepts me, has good thoughts towards me and has a good future for me. This may sound basic, but so many Christians doubt the goodness of God. They think he is angry or upset with them.

One of the most famous verses in the Bible, John 3:16, starts with 'For God so loved the world ...' God loves you and has good thoughts towards you.

> How great is the love the Father has lavished on us, that we should be called children of God! And that is what we are! (1 Jn. 3:1)

We all need to do what Psalm 34:8 says: 'Taste and see that the LORD is good; blessed is the man who takes refuge in him.'

Can you tell us how you're growing in intimacy with God? How do you connect with God in the midst of life's demands?

Keeping my walk with Jesus intimate and fresh has probably been one of my biggest challenges. The success of who you are and what you do depends upon the success of your intimacy with Jesus. The enemy understands this, and therefore the Christian's walk with God is very vulnerable. First we must be set free from the guilt of following legalistic rules. I used to be very hard on myself if I didn't read a certain number of chapters of the Bible or pray for a certain length of time. I found myself in a cycle of making commitments, being unable to keep them and then beating myself up for being a failure. God loves you and accepts whether you read 20 chapters and prayed for three hours today or not. Your acceptance comes from Christ's work on the cross, not from your own works. We are, however, called to fellowship with the Lord daily and in so doing to allow Christ to be formed in us.

I enjoy reading the Bible out loud and interacting with God as I read. I ask him questions, make comments, stop and re-read verses or sentences many times as I find them feeding my spirit. Sometimes as I read I'm reminded of another verse that is connected, so I turn and read that too. It is not how much you read that's important, but that you engage with the word. I sometimes follow times of reading with prayer, often focused on what I have just read and what has been stirred in my heart and spirit. Sometimes I read more than I pray; other times I pray more than I read. We need to be free to allow the Holy Spirit to lead us in each quiet time we have. I have also found praying in tongues to be a great source of strength in my walk with God. I try and make this a daily discipline. Jude 20 tells me to build myself up by praying in the Holy Spirit.

I have also noticed throughout the seasons of life that my heart can be cold or hot, hard or tender. I have to be proactive about keeping my heart tender before the Lord. It is my duty to keep the flame burning. I do this by periodically looking to the cross. I read the accounts of the cross and what Christ went through for me, reflect upon it and then spend time thanking him for his sacrifice for me. Reading the accounts of other men and women in history also encourages me to keep burning strong for Jesus.

With the amount of preaching I am required to do, I have found memorizing Scripture verses an invaluable discipline. It is still challenging for me, and I can do it well for a while and then not so well. But I encourage every Christian to memorize portions of the Bible. As I prepare for a series of teaching for the church I try and learn as many verses related to my subject as possible. I write them out on little pieces of card and carry them

with me. The word comes to life in me and challenges me
to live those things I am mediating upon. This gives me
power to preach it. Chuck Swindoll sums up the benefits
of memorizing Scripture:

> I know of no other single practice in the Christian
> life more rewarding, practically speaking, than
> learning Scripture. That's right. No other single
> exercise pays greater spiritual dividends. Your
> prayer life will be sharpened, your witness will
> be sharper and more effective. Your counselling
> will be in demand. Your attitudes and outlook will
> begin to change. Your mind will become more alert
> and observant. Your confidence and assurance will
> be enhanced. Your faith will be solidified.[9]

---

*What's your favourite passage in the Bible, and how are
you applying it?*

I have many favourite passages in the Bible. I usually
have a favourite for a season depending upon what the
Lord is doing in my life. At present I am living quite
strongly in Romans 8. It is too big a passage to do it
justice here. But here are two brief thoughts. The first 27
verses challenge me to live by the leading of the Holy
Spirit and not by the carnal nature. Living by the Spirit
and manifesting the nature of Christ is proof that we are
children of God. I pray frequently that the Holy Spirit
would lead me and help me to make right choices each
day.

The second half of Romans 8 encourages me by reminding me of God's goodness and of the fact that nothing
can separate me from his love. Knowing this increases
my confidence in God and his character and assures me

that he calls me and that my future is secure. I praise God for his goodness and ask for the truth of these verses to become reality in my thinking – that I will believe them more than I believe my circumstance or another person's opinion about me.

One of our biggest challenges as Christians is to believe what God says about us. People tell me what they think about me, parents have instilled into me their thoughts about me, even the enemy whispers what he thinks about me. I have to give top priority to what God says about me and believe it.

I HAVE TO GIVE TOP PRIORITY TO WHAT GOD SAYS ABOUT ME AND BELIEVE IT.

The Bible calls this renewing the mind. Renewing the mind is a continual process. The greatest battles are fought in the mind. Many contrary thoughts go through our minds, and we must allow God's word to wash our thoughts so they are obedient to Christ.

> *Steve, what one piece of wisdom from your own journey would you like to share with your fellow travellers?*

Life in Christian leadership is challenging and demanding. There are many stresses and strains and, sadly, we have more than our fair share of causalities. My first word of advice to fellow Christian leaders, and indeed to all Christians, would be to stay close to Jesus. Let's not become professional ministers but rather passionate followers of Jesus.

> So then, just as you received Christ Jesus as Lord, continue to live in him, rooted and built up in him, strengthened in the faith as you were taught, and overflowing with thankfulness. (Col. 2:6–7)

My second word of advice would be to love people – especially those closest to you. Our relationships are the most important thing we have. We need to guard and cultivate them. Love God and love people (Matt. 22:37).

Steve Uppal has brought the gospel around the UK and the world. He has worked with CfaN and currently serves as the pastor of All Nations Christian Centre in Wolverhampton. The 'three pillars' of this congregation are: overseas missions; actively engaging with all levels of the community through social action; and training and developing disciples. Steve is married to Esther. They have four children – Bethany, Sophia, Joel and Judah.

Take a moment to reflect on what you have just read. What one thing do you want to remember and apply in your own journey?

List some of the ways that you have tasted and known God's goodness in your own journey so far.

Run the Race and Finish Well

KEITH DANBY

An incredibly successful Christian businessman, Keith Danby is a man committed to the word of God, as we found out ...

> *Keith, as you reflect on your journey so far, what would you identify as some of the big life lessons God has been teaching you?*

During the past year I've been studying the book of Colossians. The first five verses have blown me away as God has given me new insight into a passage I must have read hundreds of times. These five verses contain several powerful lessons for all Christians.

Calling

In verse 1, Paul introduces himself as an apostle. An apostle is one called and set apart for the work God has for him to do. Paul had what we would call a special God moment or God crisis experience on the way to Damascus, when he saw a bright light and heard a voice, and his only response was 'what do you want me to do, Lord?' Paul would never forget this moment, when God called him into Christian service. But now, several years later, he is writing this letter from his prison cell in Rome to a small group of believers in Colossae. Had God's great plan gone wrong? Not at all. Although Paul was confined in the prison cell, in unpleasant conditions (it would have been very hot and stuffy during the day and cold and damp at night), and although he was chained to a Roman guard, he did not allow such circumstances to stop him from carrying out the call of God. He was determined to continue to serve God regardless. Neither a prison cell nor his restricted movement could stifle his work for God or cause him to question his calling.

All of us are challenged with circumstances that could, if we let them, stifle the work God has given us to do or even make us feel imprisoned. Family responsibilities, job-related stresses, financial pressures, disability, illness or infirmity, for example, could easily prevent us from having an effective ministry. Paul turned his prison cell into the mission headquarters for his ministry. What a lesson for us all to faithfully follow our calling, regardless of our situation.

> PAUL TURNED HIS PRISON CELL INTO THE MISSION HEADQUARTERS FOR HIS MINISTRY.

Citizenship

Verse 2 tells us that Paul is writing to those who are in Christ in Colossae. It struck me that we need to have dual citizenship. We have an eternal address in Christ, and an earthly address on earth. You've heard the saying that there are those who are 'so heavenly minded they're of

WE HAVE AN ETERNAL ADDRESS IN CHRIST, AND AN EARTHLY ADDRESS ON EARTH.

no earthly use'. It seems to me that if we are to be of earthly use, we must be heavenly minded. Verse 2 reminds us that each moment of each day we must live according to our dual citizenship – with one foot in heaven and the other firmly in the place where God has placed us.

Community

In verse 3, Paul talks about the importance of being part of a Christian community. 'We always thank God, the Father of our Lord Jesus Christ, when we pray for you.' We have to express our Christian commitment in community, which has three distinct strands. It has a local identity – here the community in Colossae (v. 1). Community also has a national identity – in chapters 2 and 4 Paul refers to other communities in the Lycra valley, the churches in Laodicea and the community in Hierapolis. Thirdly, community is international. The gospel is bearing fruit 'all over the world' (1:6). As Christians we are to think globally, but act locally.

Paul talks about three specific areas of ministry in relation to Christian community: people, partnership and prayer. Paul names quite a few different people in this letter. The letter is from Paul and our brother Timothy (v. 1). In verse 7, he mentions 'Epaphras, our dear fellow-servant', who brought the good news to the Colossians and also 'told us of your love in the Spirit.' In 4:7–17 he mentions ten individuals: Tychicus, Onesimus, Aristarchus, Mark, Luke, Justus, Epaphras, Demas, Nympha and Archippus. All of these people are in partnership together for the cause of the gospel. They gain strength for this purpose through their prayer – for their own work and for one another. Our calling and our citizenship has to express itself in community.

Constitution

Finally, in verse 4, Paul gives the 'Christian constitution', or the basis of our faith. It is essentially three things: faith in Christ; love for all the people; and glorious hope for the future. I need to keep all three in focus if I am to live a balanced and effective Christian life.

My life is full of meetings, travel and projects. I am learning, though, to keep all four legs of my chair firmly on the ground – my calling, my citizenship, my community and my constitution – as I use my circumstance, wherever in the world I happen to be, to fulfil my calling.

What aspect of the nature of God causes you to stand back and think, 'That's awesome!'?

God's love and forgiveness. I cannot be more loved by God than I am right now. No matter how much I mess up and wander from his purpose for my life, he is always waiting for me to return home to him, my heavenly Father. And, before I can splutter out my lines, he says, 'I love you and I forgive you. Welcome home.' As a Christian leader I am constantly aware of my failings and of my need for forgiveness for wrong attitudes, pride and arrogance. I need forgiveness for not loving people and caring for their needs as I should. I need forgiveness for thinking that my pet projects are more important than the people he has called me to serve alongside.

I CANNOT BE MORE LOVED BY GOD THAN I AM RIGHT NOW.

God's love is so amazing that he continues to strive with me and show me my shortcomings and, when I repent and turn from my wicked ways, he forgives me. Wow, what a God we have!

Can you tell us how you're growing in intimacy with God? How do you connect with God in the midst of life's demands?

I had the privilege of hearing Jerry Jenkins, the American writer and author, speak a few weeks ago. During his talk he referred to a comment that Billy Graham made when Jenkins was interviewing him for the Billy Graham biography, *Just as I Am*. Jenkins asked him, 'How have you kept your spiritual fervour and walk with the Lord fresh?' Billy Graham's response was quite profound: 'The Christian life is really quite simple – the Bible tells us to pray without ceasing and to search the Scriptures.' Dr Graham then explained that each day he tries to pray without ceasing and to have the word of God close by to read and refer to whenever he has time.

I have determined in my heart to try following that godly example and exhortation. I want to focus every spare moment in prayer and praise. I want to cultivate this practice as an attitude of mind so that, just like breathing, it becomes the most natural thing to do. I also keep the word of God handy, in my jacket pocket or in my briefcase, so when I have a few moments in between meetings, waiting for a flight or travelling on a train, I turn my attention to the Scriptures.

> *What's your favourite passage in the Bible, and how are you applying it?*

The story in John's Gospel about the feeding of the five thousand has made the biggest impact on my life. It has taught me a number of important lessons. Firstly, it reminds me that it doesn't matter how young someone is who comes to Jesus with gifts and talents. He can use them. Secondly, it doesn't matter what we have in our hand – as long as we have open hands and give whatever we have to Jesus, he can take it, bless it and use it to satisfy hungry and needy lives. Thirdly, it is always better to be part of the solution than to be part of the problem.

In Christian work it is so easy to look around and say, 'I don't have much to offer and there seem to be so many other people who are better equipped.' Instead of looking at how little we bring and thinking how inadequate it is to meet such a huge need, we need to look at Jesus and see the solution from his perspective. Each day when I go into my office and wonder

THE ANSWER IS ALWAYS JESUS, AND HE JUST WANTS ME TO HAVE AN OPEN HAND AND GIVE HIM THE LITTLE I HAVE SO HE CAN USE IT FOR HIS GLORY.

what challenges await me, I try to focus not on the problem but on the answer. The answer is always Jesus, and he just wants me to have an open hand and give him the little I have so he can use it for his glory.

> *Keith, what one piece of wisdom from your own journey would you like to share with your fellow travellers?*

Some years ago I studied the book of James. I discovered that the Greek word for perseverance is *'hypomone'*. This word is made up of two parts: the first is '*hypo*', which means 'under' (from this root we get the English word hypodermic needle, the needle that goes under the skin). The second part is '*mone*', which means 'to abide'. Put the two together and we are to abide in Christ under the circumstances of life's trials. Put it now into the context of the passage, and we understand why James says to the Christians who had fled for their lives during the persecution of the early church, 'count it all joy when you face the many coloured, uninvited trials of life that come across your path' (1:2, *The Message*). For it is through these trials that we learn to abide in Christ. It is often when we are hanging on by our fingertips in sheer desperation that we learn dependence on the Holy Spirit and how to abide in Christ in the heat of the battle.

Keith Danby is the Group Chief Executive of Send the Light Limited (STL). When he joined STL in 1987, it was part of OM and had sales revenues of £1 million and 34 volunteer staff. Now STL is a top 100 UK charity with three divisions – Authentic Media, STL Distribution and Wesley Owen Retail Group. STL has also recently established STL US and STL India. Keith sits on a number of boards, including the Evangelical Alliance and Langham Arts Trust, and he is chairman of the Bethany Hospital Trust in India.

Take a moment to reflect on what you have just read. What one thing do you want to remember and apply in your own journey?

We cannot run the race and finish well without the power that comes from God's word. How often do you turn to the Bible? Do you have it close to hand?

The Best Is Yet to Come

PENNY FRANK

Penny brings years of ministry and wisdom gleaned from her journey so far to her reflections here on God's faithfulness.

Penny, as you reflect on your journey so far, what would you identify as some of the big life lessons God has taught you?

I was born into a Christian environment and am now facing retirement, so my journey with Jesus has taken some time and covered some distance. However, I am a slow learner in spiritual things and find myself repeatedly facing the same issues and struggles. These include being true to my own principles even when others think I am wrong, having integrity in the way I live and showing kindness to those who are difficult to love. One of the most important lessons I've learned is that God never gives up on 'bringing me up'. While my parents expected

AS I GROW OLDER I FEEL MORE RESISTANT TO CHANGE – CHANGE REQUIRES ENERGY AND HUMILITY. IT BECOMES HARDER TO ADMIT I AM WRONG – OFTEN TO PEOPLE YOUNGER AND LESS EXPERIENCED THAN I AM.

to get their daughter sorted out so they could let her loose on adult life, God continues to shape and mould and teach me. His agenda is for me *never* to be independent. As I grow older I feel more resistant to change – change requires energy and humility. It becomes harder to admit I am wrong – often to people younger and less experienced than I am. Therefore it becomes even more of a challenge to confess my mistakes and to truly repent of them.

> *Can you tell us how you're growing in intimacy with God? How do you connect with God in the midst of life's demands?*

It is important to remind myself day by day that there is no coercion in God's dealings with me. It is by his love that he invites me to go on further with him – to continue to the journey's end. As he helps me to grow to be more and more like him, I am challenged to actively pursue intimacy with God. From my earliest days, I was taught that reading the Bible and praying every day were essential if I wanted to develop spiritually. But sometimes I delude myself into thinking that I know enough, or I'm tempted to study the Bible only in order to teach others. The search for intimacy with God always sends me back to his word – listening to a good Bible teacher or spending time reading a big chunk of Scripture always whets my appetite for more. There is always so much more to understand and there are so many books and tapes to help us learn. I love the Bible Speaks Today series and enjoy working my way through a book of the Bible a few verses at a time. Tom Wright's commentaries are also brilliant and accessible for personal study. I find I do need something personal. After all, I am not studying for a degree and certainly have no intention of ever writing any more essays (you heard it here!), but I need to face the challenge day by day, to live out this truth. In recent years I have realized again how eager God is to feed me and to reveal himself to me – that's wonderful.

From childhood I have enjoyed learning passages of the Bible by heart. I went to a church school and the village vicar used to come in once a week to care for our spiritual needs. Each week he would set a short passage of Scripture to learn. The reward for the person whom he considered had learned it the best was half a crown. My family always struggled financially, so this was real money for me and I always learned the passage. That vicar was not highly regarded by our family – my father was the lay leader of the village mission hall and Anglicans were hardly Christians in his eyes – but I will always be thankful to the vicar for instilling in me the habit of memorizing Scripture. I have drawn on that reservoir of memory through the years, when I have been ill or disturbed by our children in the middle of the night. I continue to learn passages now, finding their riches seep into me as I go over and over their words to store them in my memory. I also find that the truth of Scripture has far greater impact on listeners when I recite it than when I read it.

In my search for intimacy with God, worship is crucial. More and more, these times of giving God my undivided attention include extended periods of silence. I might meditate on one sentence of Scripture, or read through a well-known story and sit at the window disciplining myself to imagine the scene I have just read. In my mind I walk into the action myself and join in the conversation for a while. All of this then feeds my prayer and praise. The view of my garden, the surrounding countryside, candles on a dark early morning – these mean far more to me in my times of worship than simply providing a context for it. They focus my attention, but they also enable me to set aside a specific place for my time with God – and that has proved to be vital for me. It is this awareness of a 'holy space' that stops my mind from wandering. It stops the 'to-do lists' of the day ahead from crowding in and clamouring for attention. I also find that poetry and written prayers are a great help – as I see how people have put into words that which my own heart is struggling to say. I am an Anglican, and recently I have been using the great Collects from history. I find them so satisfying in their rich 'flavour' as they communicate huge truths and exulting worship in ordinary words. I always keep paint, crayons and paper near me on a 'quiet day' – not because I am a real artist, sadly, but because I find the visual so helpful in worshipping the invisible. I am not a great one for keeping a journal. I always have one around and record things that seem particularly significant, but I don't keep a day-to-day diary of God at work in my life. I have stopped feeling guilty about this – I just do not have time to do everything I would want to do in my daily time with God.

Over the last ten years a friend has mentored me. She welcomes me to meet with her every month for about 90 minutes and talks through the journey with me. These conversations are full of colour as we laugh, cry, talk and listen. She is full of biblical wisdom and Bible knowledge. She encourages me, challenges me, asks me just the right questions and really listens to me, and she prays for me. I have learned that God gives me some of the responsibility to make progress and to grow in strength. My own laziness would tempt me to sit back and leave this effort to someone else. A mentor's role is to ask the hard questions, offer tough encouragement and continually look for progress. Annie, who is just ahead of me on the journey, does just that. She also maintains my rootedness

A MENTOR'S ROLE IS TO ASK THE HARD QUESTIONS, OFFER TOUGH ENCOURAGEMENT AND CONTINUALLY LOOK FOR PROGRESS.

in reality. One danger of working in the national scene is that it would be easy to lose track – to forget that the local church is fundamental to the spread of the gospel and Christian growth. My ministry in my local church gives me that grass roots context that stops me being simply good at the theory. It also puts my Christian life under the spotlight as I relate and serve within the context of ordinary church life. If I lose the authenticity to serve there, then I lose my integrity as a public speaker. Our lives and witness are crippled when we fail to live out in private what we adhere to in public. My mentor ensures by her questions, prayers and observations that I maintain that 'rootedness'.

Annie is also one of the people who help me to notice how God answers prayer. That's one of God's characteristics that makes me explode 'Wow!' Yet so often I fail to take note when God is obviously at work, even when there are real specifics to take my breath away. When I miss his answers, I lose the opportunity for encouragement in my ministry and in my prayer life. Does anyone out there know exactly HOW prayer works? I don't – but when I am reminded that God hears and answers prayer then I am likely to put more effort into praying. I am also blown away that God loves and cares for me enough to listen to what I say – he hears the words 'so sorry' in my most sin-ridden moment and delights in the praise of my heart in moments of joy.

I AM ALSO BLOWN AWAY THAT GOD LOVES AND CARES FOR ME ENOUGH TO LISTEN TO WHAT I SAY – HE HEARS THE WORDS 'SO SORRY' IN MY MOST SIN-RIDDEN MOMENT AND DELIGHTS IN THE PRAISE OF MY HEART IN MOMENTS OF JOY.

I have realized over the years of my journey that praying aloud is vital for me. I need to hear my own voice making confession, expressing concern for others, putting

into words how great God is and my gratitude for Jesus.
I am aware of getting some funny looks at traffic lights
as I sit talking aloud to an empty car but who cares? My
mind is less likely to wander if I speak out loud. Listening
to songs on CD in the car also fuel my prayers if I choose
to let it – taking phrases and imagery from songs and
deliberately turning the music down or off so that I can
hear my voice speaking aloud to God.

---

*What's your favourite passage in the Bible, and how are
you applying it?*

Through this mixture of Bible reading, prayer and
mentoring, several passages of Scripture have become
peculiarly significant over the recent years. One has been
the short description in Matthew 19 of carers bringing
children to Jesus. I suppose this is not surprising as I have
spent the last forty-six years of my life bringing children
to Jesus and encouraging others to do the same. However,
over the last few years, this passage has taken on really
profound meaning for me. The scene itself seems etched
on my mind with the scruffy kids, the anxious bringers,
the protective disciples and the adamant Jesus. It's so
challenging that it was the ones closest to Jesus, not the
Pharisees nor the Romans, who tried to keep the children
away. How significant is it that Jesus neither teaches the
children, nor even tells them a story, but simply blesses
them and goes on his way? What did the children think
had happened? I would have loved to have walked back
down the hillside with them listening. In my advocacy
for children, I frequently find myself praying that the
people I meet with will hear this rebuking voice of Jesus
ringing out over their heads as they stop children coming
to him.

Another passage that has travelled with me over the last few years is Isaiah chapter 58. The chapter is actually about living for God with integrity – something I always struggle for. It is written as a poem and the lines flow with power and authenticity – here God speaks forcefully with promises of great blessing and demands for holy living. Over the years of reaching out to children I have longed to 'rebuild the broken walls' of childhood and make them 'streets to dwell in', to know the way to live as 'a well-watered garden', 'a spring of water that never fails'. God spells out the cost of that kind of fruitfulness in this passage. I have tried to be honest in my search for that productivity and to be consistent in my search for it.

Penny, if you could share just one piece of wisdom from your own journey with your fellow travellers, what would that advice be?

I HAVE LEARNED NEVER TO KID MYSELF THAT I'VE 'ARRIVED'.

I have learned never to kid myself that I've 'arrived'. I know I am a fish swimming in a small pool – the national church regarding children's ministry. I've swum around it enough times to be very familiar with it by now. People know my name in that pool and I could delude myself into thinking that I am important. It's on the mornings when that is a temptation that I need to look in the mirror and remember my sins that others don't know about, remember my weaknesses that probably rarely show through the professionalism and remember my destiny – Jesus aims at my perfection on the last day, and not before. That way I find I am thinking about Jesus and not about myself. That's much safer.

Penny Frank joined CPAS in 1987 from the teaching profession. She retired in 2005. During her years with CPAS she concentrated on children's advocacy, particularly speaking out for children with no contact with the church and therefore no chance to choose the Christian faith. She is ordained in the Anglican church and serves as a minister in her local village churches. She enjoys spending time with her two sons, daughters-in-law and four grandchildren. Their relaxation usually involves food, wine and sunshine.

Take a moment to reflect on what you have just read. What one thing do you want to remember and apply in your own journey?

Since 'the best is yet to come', try focusing today on Jesus instead of yourself. What will that look like?

Walking with Jesus

NICK LEAR

Here Nick shares his passion for Jesus, the Bible and people ...

> *Nick, as you reflect on your journey so far, what would you identify as some of the big life lessons God has been teaching you?*

This could be an extremely long list. God never stops teaching me things, even if I am not always keen to learn. However, let me share some of the biggest things that I have been learning from him more recently.

It is remarkable, considering all that he has at his disposal as King of the universe, that God chooses to use humans like you and me to fulfil his mission. It's not an accident. He relies on us to be his hands, feet, mouth and eyes with the people around us. Jesus began the process with 12 rather unlikely candidates, teaching and training them to understand his mission in the knowledge that they would fulfil it under the influence and power

JESUS HAS NO 'PLAN B'. HE CHOOSES TO USE PEOPLE BECAUSE WE ARE BEST ABLE TO SPEAK AND ACT IN WAYS THAT OTHER PEOPLE CAN RELATE TO.

of the Holy Spirit. Jesus has no 'plan B'. He chooses to use people because we are best able to speak and act in ways that other people can relate to.

The second thing that I am constantly aware of is that relying on God is not easy. He gives us all a wide range of gifts, intelligence and talents to use in life and in his service, but my natural tendency is to rely on them, rather than the One who gave them to me. That tendency makes about as much sense as having a computer with the fastest processor chips and the most impressive graphics, but failing to plug it into the electricity supply and wondering why it's not working.

Finally, God is continually reminding me that a sense of humour is one of the most important gifts that humans have. Laughing is healthy for our bodies, and a sense of humour enables us to look at the difficulties of life from a slightly different perspective. I should laugh more and frown less. That does not mean we make fun of other people, but seeing the lighter side of life enables us to lift our eyes up from our problems and, as we do that, it gives God the chance to show us his perspective on things.

> *What aspect of the nature of God causes you to stand back and think, 'That's awesome!'?*

I am addicted to Jesus. I love reading about him in the Bible: seeing what he did, exploring what he said and trying to follow him. But the most amazing thing about him was his unconditional love, which ultimately led him to die for me. Whatever I do I can never make God love me any less or any more. His

EVEN WHEN I MESS UP, GOD STILL LOVES ME AS MUCH AS WHEN I FEEL REALLY CLOSE TO HIM.

love for me is always at its maximum possible level. That means I don't have to try to earn his love – it's always there. Even when I mess up, God still loves me as much as when I feel really close to him.

Can you tell us how you're growing in intimacy with God? How do you connect with God in the midst of life's demands?

It is essential for my spiritual health that I regularly read the Bible. I don't find that the discipline of a regular 'quiet time' works for me, but I make sure that my Bible is nearby so I can pick it up and read it during the day when I get a moment. I love reading familiar passages and hearing God say something new to me. I also love finding new parts of the Bible that I haven't explored yet. I get to know Jesus best when I am involved in his word. His Spirit inspired its writing and he inspires its reading now.

IT IS ESSENTIAL FOR MY SPIRITUAL HEALTH THAT I REGULARLY READ THE BIBLE.

I also try to make space to chat with Jesus as I do everyday things. He is always with me by his Spirit, and it seems impolite to limit my conversations to a quick time in the morning or evening. When I am alone in my car I like to put a worship album in the CD player, turn it up loud and sing my lungs out to Jesus. I get some funny looks, but that doesn't matter. I arrive at the end of a journey having spent some serious quality time with Jesus. (It's good for road rage, too!)

I need to spend more time listening to God, being quiet on my own and asking him to speak. On the occasions that I do this, I am always amazed at what God says. I sit or lie down quietly and, after becoming aware of any distractions, I focus on asking God what he wants to say. This is how I hear from him most clearly. When one thought seems to be more important than most and seems to be from Jesus I repeat it over and over again, allowing it to become part of me. Praying with other people is brilliant, as well. It helps me to focus on other people's needs, and not just my own, and God often speaks to me in those moments too. This is one of the privileges of my job – in most meetings I have with people they are happy to pray with me.

What's your favourite passage in the Bible, and how are you applying it?

I love the Bible. All of it. Even the bits that are difficult to understand. It is such an amazing book that selecting a favourite bit is a little like asking me to decide which of my senses is my favourite. If I had to narrow it down I would probably select two parts of the Bible. I love Jesus' parables – they communicate God's truth so powerfully. They are entertaining (especially if you are able to appreciate Jesus' sense of humour in many of them), and the Spirit uses them to explain great truths about Jesus and what it means to follow him. If I was pushed to select just one favourite biblical passage, it would be the resurrection account in Luke 24. Jesus' resurrection is God having the last laugh after the devil thought he had written the punch-line, and it is amazing to watch the bewildered disciples gradually realize what had happened and then explode with joy. What a day!

In addition to reminding me of the thrill of knowing that I follow a risen Saviour, not a dead prophet, Luke 24 cautions me that I should never think I understand God completely. It took the disciples a long time to believe that

Jesus was alive, even though he had been telling them about it for weeks before his death. Even when the women told the disciples what they had seen, and some of them had seen the empty tomb, they still 'went away, wondering ... what had happened' (v. 12).

Then there's Cleopas and his unnamed companion, walking back to Emmaus from Jerusalem. These two people ought to have known better, but they failed to recognize Jesus visually or through his teaching. There is great comic timing here – they spend a whole journey with him, invite him to stay, and the instant they recognize Jesus he disappears. So then they run all the way back to Jerusalem, burst in through the door where the rest of the disciples are staying, and just as they relate what has happened Jesus appears in their midst. It is a healthy lesson in humility to realize that I know far less about Jesus than they did, and to realize that I need to listen to him. It also reminds me to expect the unexpected with Jesus.

> *Nick, what one piece of wisdom from your own journey would you like to share with your fellow travellers?*

In a word, 'encourage'! Human nature is such that we take more notice of criticism than we do encouragements. It is easy to become discouraged by what other people say. When they say nothing, I wonder whether I am doing a good job. A wise lecturer at Bible college advised me to have an encouragement file, keeping letters and cards that people occasionally give me to say 'thank you'. If I get discouraged or doubt that Jesus is using me, I open the file, read some of the things people have said and get a 'well done, good and faithful servant' from

IN A WORD, 'ENCOURAGE'!

Jesus. A couple of them have also found their way into my Bible so that I come across them more often. It may sound conceited, but the purpose is not to make me big-headed. If people have taken the time and trouble to encourage me, it seems to be a good use of that encouragement to make it last longer than just that one moment.

As I recognize my own need for encouragement, I also try to encourage others, to take the time to say 'thank you' to as many people as I can so that they get the same message from Jesus through me. This is not just good for someone's ego or for team morale. This encouragement could be exactly what someone needs to hear from God at that moment, and I believe God wants all of us to be involved in this. I'm not brilliant at it, but if I can look for positive things that others have done and tell them about it then I believe God can speak to them through me – which blesses both of us.

Nick is married to Sally and they have two children, Thomas and Hannah. He became a Christian at the age of six and was baptized at thirteen. He works as a mission adviser for the Baptist Union of Great Britain, advising churches on youth and children's work.

Take a moment to reflect on what you have just read. What one thing do you want to remember and apply in your own journey?

How can you be more proactive about encouraging others in their walk with Jesus?

Persevering with God:
Over the Years and Around the World

STANLEY DAVIES

The story of Stanley's journey reflects many of the movements of God throughout the world over the past half-century.

My life's journey began in 1939 in India, where my parents were missionaries. When I was four years old my family returned to the UK on board a troop ship in convoy. That was a pretty rough way to travel. When we travelled through the stormy Red Sea the captain apparently said that he was glad for the conditions, as they made it difficult for the German U-boats to operate. We docked safely in the Clyde close to Glasgow, ending the first of my many journeys – both physical and spiritual.

As I look back, I see that one of the big life lessons God has been teaching me is that he is in control of all circumstances and plans. I have discovered that my responsibility is to listen and learn from him and follow his directions.

This was true during my business days as a young cartographical surveyor, when I travelled throughout the UK and then internationally. I met some wonderful people who helped me on my journey and guided me in following Jesus.

When I was seventeen I had tea in the home of the Persian General Secretary of the Bible Society in Terhan, Iran, before the fall of the Shah of Persia. At eighteen I was in the Sudan mapping the site of the Roseires Dam on the Blue Nile. There I met up with SIM missionaries who were a great encouragement to me in a desolate place. Shortly after that, I went to Nigeria to prepare maps for the Kainji Dam on the River Niger. While I was there I received a telegram saying that my youngest sister had died while undergoing an operation on her kidney. Some local missionaries comforted me and stood by me.

When I was nineteen I visited Afghanistan and surveyed the route for a new road from Kabul to Kandahar. While in Kabul I worshipped at the Kabul Christian Community Church and was given a welcome text by the pastor, Dr Christy Wilson: Isaiah 40:3. 'In the desert prepare the way for the LORD; make straight in the wilderness a highway for our God.' This turned out to be a key life text for me. John the Baptist, who saw that these words applied to himself, quoted them (Jn. 1:23). Later John spoke some words that have repeatedly challenged me, and that continue to challenge me each day: 'He must become greater; I must become less.' In all I have sought to be and do I have tried to follow John's example.

After all of this international travel I received a letter from Her Majesty the Queen asking me to join her forces – I was one of the last to get called up for National Service. I joined the Royal Engineers and was commissioned at Chatham at the age of twenty. My posting was to Kenya to lead a squadron of sappers (army slang for the Royal Engineers) in the last years of the colonial administration of that country. During my time there Kenya experienced extremes of weather – from severe drought to damaging floods in many parts of the country. Providing famine relief to needy areas, rebuilding bridges and reconstructing roads and airfields were all part of our assignment. I later discovered that this was all part of God's preparation for future service for him.

During those two years in the military I linked up with the Officers Christian Union as well as SASRA, both Christian organizations serving the British military forces. They were a great help and encouragement to me. I also appreciated the ministry of the MMG club, where I found a Christian base as an oasis in the army desert.

My faith was tested many times during the fourteen months I spent in Kenya – in the officers' mess as well as on assignments in the country. A particularly testing time came when my Squadron of Royal Engineers was posted to Kuwait for three months as part of the UK military force sent in to keep General Kassem and his Iraqi troops from invading Kuwait. It was a barren time spiritually during which I was isolated from Christian fellowship.

While in Kenya I linked up with missionaries from the Africa Inland Mission and was able to attend some of their conferences and visit them in different parts of the country. In Lokori, among the Turkana people in the north of the country, I met Dr Dick Anderson and his wife, Joan, who were pioneer missionaries in that vast region.

During these years of international travel I learned the importance of Christian fellowship, both as a means of encouragement and learning for myself, as well as an opportunity to declare my witness as a follower of Jesus to those with whom I was working.

On concluding my National Service I returned to the UK and married my fiancée, Margaret, who had trained as a nurse and midwife. As both of us shared a love for Jesus as well as a growing conviction that we should prepare ourselves for Christian service, within a couple of months of marrying we moved to Scotland to attend the Bible Training Institute in Glasgow.

Those two years of Bible and missionary training were challenging and enriching in all sorts of ways. Making long-term friendships with fellow students who would serve the Lord in countries all over the world was a key part of being in a community of people eager to learn of God's word and his world. Learning new skills and lessons under the supervision of godly trainers was a huge benefit in preparing for service in God's world. At the beginning of our second year there we welcomed Andrew, our first child, into the world.

During our time in Glasgow we sought God's will for our lives. We had a growing conviction that he wanted us to serve him somewhere beyond the UK, but discovering where he wanted us to go and with which agency was more difficult to discern. This took time and many conversations. In the end we applied to serve with the Africa Inland Mission in Kenya and were accepted for service there.

I returned to Kenya as a servant of the King of kings rather than as a soldier of Her Majesty the Queen. This time I was accompanied by a wife and two baby boys. Our second son, Philip, had been born a few months earlier. Our first assignment was to learn Kalenjin, a language spoken by seven related tribes in the west central area of the country. This proved a challenging task, as it is a tonal language and a slightly raised or lowered inflection can result in one saying something very different from what was intended. We also helped to build a basic conference centre on the site where we were staying – and my engineering experience was in demand.

After six months of language study we moved to Kapsowar, in Marakwet District, where we were assigned to general missionary work including evangelism, church work, school supervision and the care of the infrastructure and superstructure of a rural hospital that had been established 30 years previously. This latter assignment included supervising the water supply from a nearby river, caring for an old diesel engine that supplied electricity and maintaining the existing buildings and designing and erecting new ones. Again, God was using my engineering experience. While we were there our daughter, Carol, was born in Eldoret Hospital. Over a 15-year period we took on a range of assignments in youth work, training, discipleship and leadership.

It was a privilege to work alongside Kenyan pastors and elders in the churches of the district. As young missionaries, we appreciated their gracious guidance and help as we continued to learn the language and culture of the area while serving the needs of the area as best we could.

Later we moved to Nairobi to work as acting Field Secretary for the three hundred AIM missionaries in Kenya. There our youngest son, Tim, was born. During this period the Africa Inland Church was going through major changes as it took responsibility for all the departments of the mission that had been developed – literature, medical work, education, theological education and many more.

Following the serious illness of the principal of Scott Theological College at Machakos, I became emergency principal. Although we were able to meet particular needs in all of these different assignments, at times we wondered why the mission kept moving us. I can see now, however, how the Lord was preparing me for future work with a breadth of experience that would have been impossible to gain if we had stayed in any one location or ministry.

In 1980 we moved back to the UK to care for our parents who were ill and needed our support. This un-expected development meant seeking the Lord for a new assignment, and I became Director of Mission Studies at Moorlands Bible College. We moved to Dorset for three years with the understanding that when our parents no longer needed us we would return to Kenya with AIM. Not being a trained teacher, I was stretched to develop new courses for those preparing for mission service. However the college required an experienced missionary for the post, rather than someone who had plenty of academic credentials without the experience. I learned a great deal from my fellow lecturers and from the students. I had learned a bit about contemporary British culture from our three teenagers, who had been at boarding school in the UK for several years, but moving back here provided me with a full crash course on a culture that had changed dramatically while we had been away. During this time both my mother and mother-in-law died.

As our three years at Moorlands drew to a close we received an unexpected call to a completely new assignment with the Evangelical Missionary Alliance. They wanted to appoint their first full-time general secretary, following the retirement of their part-time secretary Ernest Oliver. Accepting this post meant moving to London, where the EMA office was based, as well as saying goodbye to returning to Kenya.

Guidance doesn't appear to get any easier as we get older and perhaps become more sceptical and less trusting of our own ideas. After much heart searching we accepted this as the Lord's leading and moved to London. EMA solved our housing problem by providing us with a 50% equity share in buying a property, and we were able to get a mortgage on the rest. Thus God graciously enabled us to get a step on the property ladder so that, when I retired 21 years later, we could purchase a house in Leicester with half the proceeds of the sale of the

GUIDANCE DOESN'T APPEAR TO GET ANY EASIER AS WE GET OLDER AND PERHAPS BECOME MORE SCEPTICAL AND LESS TRUSTING OF OUR OWN IDEAS.

house in London. Once again, we saw God fulfilling his promise to guide and provide for all our needs.

The work at EMA was demanding as we sought to encourage mission agencies and colleges to face up to changes around the world. Many member agencies had been established in the late nineteenth century and had done great things in the areas of the world where they had operated. At the end of the twentieth century, however, they faced very different situations both abroad and in the UK. The length of time a missionary spent abroad was being drastically reduced. The role of missionaries in countries where churches had been planted had changed significantly. There was also significant growth in short-term mission initiatives.

Agencies that chose to support different aspects of mission rather than send UK missionaries began to proliferate. Some sent money to developing churches, others chose to specialize in theological education, Bible translation, literature, radio and other media. The influx of immigrants from commonwealth countries brought new challenges to the majority white Christians of the UK who had always perceived 'mission' to be overseas rather than in the UK.

British Christians were also seeking new ways to respond to the overwhelming humanitarian needs around the world. The establishment of agencies like Tearfund and World Vision, as well as agencies such as Open Doors that sought to help persecuted Christians, encouraged involvement in new ways – other than sending UK missionaries to the ends of the earth.

EMA itself faced up to the changing world and, after careful study, re-launched itself under the name 'Global Connections', which sought to be more inclusive of all parties in the UK involved in global mission. This included local churches and Christians in business travelling internationally as well as the agencies and colleges that had been members of EMA.

One aspect of the work of Global Connections was to engage with others in Europe and around the world who were also involved in cross-cultural mission – through umbrella organizations like the European Evangelical Missionary Alliance and the World Evangelical Alliance Mission Commission. It was thrilling to see how the Lord of the harvest was calling Brazilians and Koreans, Indians and Nigerians, and many from other nations around the world as well, to be involved in the mission of God to the nations. It is essential, at the start of the twenty-first century, both to share our experience as an older sending nation and to learn from new sending nations. I have been tremendously enriched and challenged as I have met with mission leaders from around the world.

During my years at EMA/Global Connections I was conscious of the need to be vigilant against the attacks of Satan on my person and ministry. Often those attacks were launched against different members of my family. Serious illness affected two members of my immediate family. I sensed these were not just physical, but spiritual attacks on our ministry. Then my eldest son, aged twenty-seven, dropped dead at work. Where was God in all of this? I asked. In the darkness of a very long tunnel it was hard to discern the presence of God. Yet he never forsook me. He was always there, even when I could not feel his presence. It was a hard, long struggle to trust in the dark when doubts came flooding in and faith was weak and faltering. In those times I had to learn new lessons from my Lord.

Maintaining a close walk with the Lord in a busy world takes determination to make

MAINTAINING A CLOSE WALK WITH THE LORD IN A BUSY WORLD TAKES DETERMINATION TO MAKE TIME FOR GOD AND HIS WORD.

time for God and his word. Through my years in ministry I recognized that this did not happen automatically – I had to make it a priority. As a young surveyor in Afghanistan, the only quiet time and place I could find was walking in the fields close to our campsite early in the morning or just before sunset, away from my surveying colleagues whose conversation was laced with expletives. During my time in the military I had to discipline myself to make time to be alone with God. This meant choosing not to be involved in some of the activities of those around me as they would have prevented me from spending time with God. Other times, it meant avoiding activities that would have compromised my Christian faith.

Over all the years of my Christian ministry I had to determine when and where I would find a time and place to read God's word and spend time in adoration and intercession. This was a perpetual battle that I often failed to win.

One lesson I have learned is that God takes the weak things of the world to confound the wise. It is when we discover our own weakness that we begin to rely more and more on him. 'Power through weakness' is perhaps the greatest lesson I have learned in all my years of business, travel and mission. It is incredible that the mighty eternal God, who made the universe, is interested in me. That I belong to him is all of his mercy and grace. Anything that I have done is all because of his power and enabling.

'POWER THROUGH WEAKNESS' IS PERHAPS THE GREATEST LESSON I HAVE LEARNED IN ALL MY YEARS OF BUSINESS, TRAVEL AND MISSION.

 Stanley Davies is honorary president of Global Connections (formerly the Evangelical Missionary Alliance), a trustee and chairman of InterHealth and chairman of the council of All Nations Christian College.

Take a moment to reflect on what you have just read. What one thing do you want to remember and apply in your own journey?

What does it mean for you, at this point in your faith journey, to persevere with God?

Pilgrims Only: No Prizes for Tourists

JOEL EDWARDS

Influential Christian leader, author, broadcaster and the first black director in the Evangelical Alliance's 150-year history, Joel Edwards maps out the course of his journey so far – and the course of God's faithfulness.

All of us have a ministry, and for each of us the route into God's purposes is as unique as the combination of circumstances which make up our lives. But however we get there – or find ourselves getting there – three things are constant. First, there is only one Route Master and one destination. Second, when we get there all of us will give an account not for the route we took but how we maximized the journey. Third, there are no prizes for tourists – only for pilgrims.

And, what's more, we are all servants along the journey. As we travel on our individual journeys we share and compare our stories, but we never compete. I hope you will find something in the story of my journey so far that will encourage you as God leads you on your own journey.

SOMEWHERE IN THE TOP TRAY OF LESSONS LEARNED IS THE FACT THAT NOTHING STARTS BIG.

Somewhere in the top tray of lessons learned is the fact that nothing starts big.

Whatever I'm doing now began back in my earliest days as a very small church mouse in Kingston, Jamaica.

For as long as I can remember, Christian worship has been central to my world. I may have been five or six years old, but if I close my eyes I can still see them – happy, featureless faces dressed in their Sunday best. Worshipping giants towering above me. Trumpets and tambourines, hand clapping and stomping feet. Sweats of joy. And Elder Shaw. If I slept, he would wake me in my mother's arms. But it always seemed a great way to be woken up. For, even then, I knew that what he was saying was so worth shouting about that I wanted to be a part of it. Or maybe I already was? This was New Town Church.

I have no idea what Elder Shaw said, but it must have been true. Somewhere between the ages of five and six I decided that preaching was the greatest sound in the world. All of that carried over into church life in Britain. I could never have imagined just how much Sunday School and youth choir days prepared me for the future. And Sister McKenzie.

I often talk about 'Sister Mc', for more than anyone else she truly discipled me. 'Sister Mc' was often very strict, but her persistence and genuine love for us won through. I learned my social skills in the unspectacular environment of Sister McKenzie's youth choir and Sunday School classes. It was a carefree, mischievous adolescence punctuated with adult restraints. A belly full of laughs which Sister McKenzie interrupted with real work from time to time.

I had no idea at the time but, in my journey, Sister McKenzie was my most significant coach.

From the age of eight, as a young 'coloured boy' in Britain I learned to dance between cultures, crossing boundaries between Christian Caribbeanisms and secular Britain. I had to learn to navigate a course between my small but vital world and my expanding world – where I was one of three Christians and one of four Black pupils in a school of 1,200 boys. Christian strength helped me to figure out both worlds. By trial and error I developed survival skills in sharing my unusual Christian world in a tough school environment where they couldn't be bothered to teach us French in the second year, a pupil chased the gym teacher with a Stanley knife, the headmaster had a breakdown and I emerged as the first Black Christian School Captain. As Captain I had to balance the privilege of representing my school at the local Rotary Club with the fact that I received free school meals and uniforms. Bizarre.

But God has also taught me that my past does not necessarily determine my future.

In my past, carefree days in the heat of the Caribbean sun mingle with memories of abuse. I wasn't the one abused: it was my mother. One Monday morning when I was about six years old, I woke up to find that my mother had left Jamaica, without warning, to travel to Britain. It was a desperate attempt to escape the suffocating abuse of my father. Etched in my childhood memories are the beatings and my mother's helpless wailings.

I was in my late forties when she told me the story of how she had left home for church the day before with my eldest sister. She told my sister she was leaving for England and sent her back to our house with the secret. She then caught a flight later that day. There were five of us children and, apart from my eldest sister, she left without saying goodbye to any of us. She had to.

That was a terrible Monday morning.

It was two years before I joined her in England – the mother country about which I sang everyday with the Union Jack in the corner of my classroom in Jamaica. I have never known what it's like to have two parents living together in harmony under the same roof. And growing up in a single-parent family meant that I never knew the guidance of a father.

Perhaps, on reflection, those circumstances contributed to my petty crime career as a Woolworth's thief. Despite the fact that I was regularly in church, the habit went on for some time before I was caught and put on probation. Hitting rock-bottom was a spiritual HITTING ROCK-BOTTOM WAS A SPIRITUAL WAKE-UP CALL. wake-up call. My world stopped when they put me in that cell. My mother died a thousand deaths when she came to collect me from the police. But God wasn't phased by it.

And here's my biggest lesson about God: timing is everything, and God is pretty good at it.

Ideas about 'ministry' had always lurked in the back of my mind, but they took on a new sense of urgency when I was between the ages of sixteen and nineteen. By this time Sister McKenzie's efforts and my own gifting were becoming evident. I was leading a gospel band and playing a central role in large worship settings, comfortable in presenting short sermons and active in youth ministries.

But I had a hunger for something more. When I was nineteen, a most amazing thing happened. During an evening service there was an incredible sense of God's presence. And during that service I became overwhelmed by buckets of love which seemed to pour through me and emerged in worship in a language I had never learned. We called it the 'baptisms of the Holy Spirit'. It was not an emotional charge. It was a surcharge of love which made everything lovable and produced in me an insatiable appetite for the Bible.

In 1972 I went to London Bible College to do a degree in theology. My three years there were to prove the most formative for my future work. It wasn't just that I learned about the Bible. It was much more to do with what I learned about myself. For one thing, I learned that there were other people who loved God and understood him far better than I had. This was revelation. I had always suspected that people from other churches might also have unhindered access to God, but it was only a hunch. During these three years I learned humility as I discovered that God has a lot more friends than I thought he was allowed to keep. It was a big kingdom with many pilgrims on its narrow path. I learned to share the space with them.

Before attending LBC (now the London School of Theology) I had no idea what the word 'evangelical' meant. I met brilliant scholars, discovered new ways of reading the Bible and forged friendships which were investments for future work. Had anyone suggested to me in those heady days that I would one day emerge as a leader in the evangelical world I would never have believed it. In any event I can't imagine who would have made such a suggestion.

When I left LBC in 1975 I had a range of options available to me for which I had not fully developed skills, including work as a probationary officer and pastoring a church for ten years.

My exposure to a wider world of church turned out to be a part of a master plan. In 1988 I was appointed as the first general secretary of the African and Caribbean Evangelical Alliance – an umbrella body which works across the range of Black majority churches in Britain. My four years with ACEA opened the door to serving the wider church. In 1992 my work with the Evangelical Alliance began with my appointment as UK director. I worked to build partnerships and serve a wide network of member organizations before my appointment as general director in 1997. None of this was planned – it has all been a part of the journey.

All of this has been a kind of Emmaus journey (Luke 24:28). Walking with a friend. No day passes without a sense of God's presence. Frankly, my journey has not been marked by unbroken patterns of daily Bible studies and meditations. But life would be inconceivable without a sense of his presence, and ministry would be unimaginable without his nearness. I do not always experience 'intimacy' with God, but I live in perpetual awareness of him. Without this awareness I would be totally ruined, for it keeps me focused even in those times when I do not feel that intimacy. Those are the times of questionings, uncertainties and the arguments he always wins. Sooner or later that awareness of God inevitably reignites intimacy with him.

> BUT LIFE WOULD BE INCONCEIVABLE WITHOUT A SENSE OF HIS PRESENCE, AND MINISTRY WOULD BE UNIMAGINABLE WITHOUT HIS NEARNESS.

That awareness also guides my attitudes to the Bible. I'm always wary of choosing 'my favourite Bible text'. Over the years many texts have seemed particularly pertinent at various times before receding in importance in order to make room for others. They include passages such as Psalms 121, 51 and 61. There was a period in my early ministry when I became totally saturated in Psalm 23. As a pastor, I posted Ezra 7:10 on the wall of my study for some time. I have been transfixed by Christ's sonship in Hebrews 1:1–3.

Like most Christians, I have no difficulty in turning to the Scriptures for consolation in times of trouble or deep anxiety. But increasingly I like to think of the Bible as a mobile phone calling for my attention. The Caller's name is always on display on this phone. The challenge is to decide whether I am too busy to answer it or whether I am willing to be challenged by the conversation which will ensue. And, even when I have to catch up with my reading, there is nothing like those times when God speaks directly to me from the Bible as I open myself up to my 'unopened messages'. However busy I become, the word is always waiting.

In this precarious, exciting and exhilarating journey, how else could I possibly stay on course?

 Rev Joel Edwards is the General Director of the Evangelical Alliance UK. Joel's vision is to see the church become a movement for change, bringing biblical transformation to society. Joel is also an accomplished broadcaster and author. His most recent book is *Hope, Respect and Trust – Valuing These Three* (Milton Keynes: Authentic Lifestyle, 2004). He is married to Carol, and they have two grown children.

Take a moment to reflect on what you have just read. What one thing do you want to remember and apply in your own journey?

Have you ever felt like a tourist on your journey with God?
What are the differences between pilgrims and tourists?

Your Journey so Far ...

As you reflect on your journey so far, what would you identify as some of the big life lessons God has been teaching you?

What title might you use for your reflections on your journey so far?

What aspect of the nature of God causes you to stand back and think, 'That's awesome!'?

The contributors to this volume were particularly struck by many different characteristics of God. Which of their experiences helped you to appreciate something about God in a new or fresh way?

How are you growing in intimacy with God? How do you connect with God in the midst of life's demands?

Will you experiment with any of the different ways of developing intimacy with God suggested in this book? Which ones?

What is your favourite passage in the Bible? How are you applying it?

Why do you think so many people are reflecting on the significance of Isaiah 58?

What one piece of wisdom from your own journey would you like to share with your fellow travellers? (With whom will you share this wisdom and when?)

Crusaders in the Twenty-first Century

Crusaders is a missionary movement passionate about empowering every child and young person to fulfil his or her God-given potential. The primary role of the movement is to envision, equip, empower and encourage the many thousands of volunteer leaders who faithfully reach out to this generation – every day, every week, every month, every year.

Crusaders' 'Energize' package of resources and training materials equips leaders to walk young people from childhood to adulthood by providing flexible weekly meeting plans, drama sketches, monthly articles, regional training days and distance learning training tools. Crusaders also offers a comprehensive range of events including residential short-term service and mentoring opportunities for young people.

For more specific information on 'Energize' contact Crusaders' Ministry Support team on 01582 589840, e-mail at energize@crusaders.org.uk, or check out the website on www.crusaders.org.uk/energize (where there are free samples!).

Endnotes

[1] Josh McDowell, *His Image, My Image* (Milton Keynes: Authentic Media, 2005). *See Yourself as God Sees You* (Carol Stream, IL: Tyndale House, 1999).

[2] Gary Thomas, *Sacred Pathways: Discover Your Soul's Path to God* (Grand Rapids, MI: Zondervan, 2002), page 18.

[3] Thomas, *Sacred Pathways*, page 46.

[4] Thomas, *Sacred Pathways*, page 139.

[5] Thomas, *Sacred Pathways*, page 215.

[6] Thomas, *Sacred Pathways*, page 219.

[7] Philip Yancey, *What's so Amazing about Grace?* (Grand Rapids, MI: Zondervan, 1997), page 30.

[8] Charles Swindoll, *The Grace Awakening* (Nashville, TN: Thomas Nelson, 2003).

[9] In Donald S. Whitney, *Spiritual Disciplines for the Christian Life* (Colorado Springs, CO: NavPress, 1997).